Table of Contents

Unit 1
Language and Usage: The Sentence

Unit 2
Literature and Writing: Personal Narrative   11

Unit 3
Language and Usage: Nouns   17

Unit 4
Literature and Writing: Comparison and Contrast   23

Unit 5
Language and Usage: Verbs   29

Unit 6
Literature and Writing: Story   45

Unit 7
Language and Usage: Modifiers   51

Unit 8
Literature and Writing: Description   57

Unit 9
Mechanics: Capitalization and Punctuation   63

Unit 10
Literature and Writing: Persuasive Letter   75

Unit 11
Language and Usage: Pronouns   81

Unit 12
Literature and Writing: Research Report   89

Unit 13
Language and Usage: Phrases   97

Unit 14
Language and Usage: Clauses   107

Teacher's Annotated Pages

Unit 1
Language and Usage: The Sentence   T1

Unit 2
Literature and Writing: Personal Narrative   T6

Unit 3
Language and Usage: Nouns — **T9**

Unit 4
Literature and Writing: Comparison and Contrast — **T11**

Unit 5
Language and Usage: Verbs — **T14**

Unit 6
Literature and Writing: Story — **T22**

Unit 7
Language and Usage: Modifiers — **T25**

Unit 8
Literature and Writing: Description — **T28**

Unit 9
Mechanics: Capitalization and Punctuation — **T30**

Unit 10
Literature and Writing: Persuasive Letter — **T36**

Unit 11
Language and Usage: Pronouns — **T39**

Unit 12
Literature and Writing: Research Report — **T43**

Unit 13
Language and Usage: Phrases — **T47**

Unit 14
Language and Usage: Clauses — **T52**

Index — **T56**

Name _____   **RETEACHING WORKBOOK** 5

LANGUAGE AND USAGE

5 | Compound Subjects and Compound Predicates

> ▶ A **compound subject** is made up of two or more simple subjects.
> ▶ A **compound predicate** is made up of two or more simple predicates.
>
> **Compound Subject:**   People, animals, and plants inhabit the earth.
> **Compound Predicate:** Do they live, grow, and thrive everywhere?

Write the simple subjects or simple predicates that are joined by each underlined conjunction.

Example: Scientists have discovered and named many kinds of animals.

   have discovered, named _____

1. No continent or ocean lacks living things. _____

2. Plants and animals are important to the environment.

   _____

3. Green plants provide food and give off oxygen. _____

4. Neither yeast plants nor mold plants are green, however.

   _____

5. Mold seeds float in the air, settle on food, and grow into plants.

   _____

6. Plants rely on and enrich the soil. _____

7. Air and water are necessary for survival. _____

8. Many scientists collect soil samples and analyze the contents.

   _____

9. Some scientists study plants but may not work outside a lab.

   _____

10. Do ecologists or astronomers study our environment?

   _____

Level 8 Unit 1 **The Sentence**   *(Use with pupil book pages 22–23.)*
Skill: Students will identify compound subjects and compound predicates.

Name _____ RETEACHING WORKBOOK **6**

LANGUAGE AND USAGE

6 | Combining Sentences: Compound Sentences

▶ You can combine two or more related sentences into a **compound sentence.** Join the sentences with a conjunction. Add a comma before the conjunction.

Simple Sentences:	Foxes are wild animals. Some live in big cities.
Compound Sentence:	Foxes are wild animals, **but** some live in big cities.
Simple Sentences:	Can you approach a fox? Is it too dangerous?
Compound Sentence:	Can you approach a fox, **or** is it too dangerous?

Write each pair of sentences as one compound sentence. Use the conjunction in parentheses, and add a comma where needed.

Example: Foxes are clever animals. They are skillful hunters.   **(and)**

Foxes are clever animals, and they are skillful hunters.

1. Foxes are related to wolves. They are smarter than wolves.   **(but)**

   _____

2. A female fox is a vixen. A young fox is called a pup.   **(and)**

   _____

3. A baby fox needs its parents' care. It will not survive.   **(or)**

   _____

4. Foxes play an important role. Farmers depend on them.   **(and)**

   _____

5. Foxes eat mice. Mice eat farmers' crops.   **(and)**

   _____

6. The red fox lives mainly on rodents. It will eat anything.   **(but)**

   _____

7. Have you seen a fox in the woods? Have you just seen pictures?   **(or)**

   _____

8. A fox may look like a dog. Never mix up the two!   **(but)**

   _____

Level 8 Unit 1   The Sentence   *(Use with pupil book pages 24–25.)*
Skill: Students will form compound sentences.

Name _____

RETEACHING WORKBOOK 7

LANGUAGE AND USAGE

7 | Conjunctions

> ▶ **Coordinating conjunctions** join words or groups of words.
> ▶ **Correlative conjunctions** are used in pairs to join words or groups of words.
>
> **Coordinating Conjunctions:** and, but, or, nor, for, yet
> **Correlative Conjunctions:** either . . . or   both . . . and
>   neither . . . nor   not only . . . but (also)

Write the coordinating or correlative conjunctions in each sentence.

Example: Painting is an old and important art form.   **and**

1. An artist expresses ideas or presents feelings in a personal way.   _____

2. People paint realistic scenes or abstracts.   _____

3. Either the first method or the second can produce a beautiful painting.   _____

4. Not only shapes but also colors are important in a painting.   _____

5. Both children and adults can paint.   _____

6. Painting is easy, but painting well is not.   _____

7. Many artists work long hours, for they are perfectionists.   _____

8. Some painters will not tire, nor will they give up.   _____

9. An artist's life is difficult yet satisfying.   _____

10. Neither fame nor wealth comes to many artists.   _____

11. The joy and satisfaction are what count.   _____

12. Children and adults admire paintings in museums.   _____

13. Museums not only have displays but also offer tours.   _____

14. Visitors may ask questions or offer comments.   _____

Level 8   Unit 1   The Sentence   *(Use with pupil book pages 26–27.)*
Skill: Students will identify coordinatng and correlative conjunctions.

Houghton Mifflin English 8
Copyright © Houghton Mifflin Company. All rights reserved.

Name _____

RETEACHING WORKBOOK 8

LANGUAGE AND USAGE

8 | Complex Sentences

▶ An **independent clause** can stand alone.
▶ A **subordinate clause** cannot stand alone and usually begins with a subordinating conjunction.
▶ A **complex sentence** has an independent clause and one or more subordinate clauses.

        subordinate clause   independent clause
Because they grow in all climates, trees are found almost everywhere.

      independent clause   subordinate clause
Trees are found almost everywhere **because they grow in all climates.**

Write the subordinate clause in each complex sentence.

Example: Whereas some trees have many uses, others are simply beautiful.
        Whereas some trees have many uses

1. There are more kinds of trees than you can imagine.

    _____

2. The odd-shaped Joshua tree grows in the desert where most plants cannot live.

    _____

3. Whenever people see the tree, they notice its dagger-shaped leaves.

    _____

4. The flowering peach tree should have a different name since it produces no peaches.

    _____

5. Many people imagine otherwise because it has this misleading name.

    _____

6. The sausage tree sounds tasty although its fruit is not edible.

    _____

7. As you might expect, the flowers of the pocket-handkerchief tree look like handkerchiefs.

    _____

Level 8 Unit 1 The Sentence   *(Use with pupil book pages 28–30.)*
Skill: Students will identify subordinate clauses in complex sentences.

Name _____   RETEACHING WORKBOOK

LANGUAGE AND USAGE

9 | Correcting Fragments and Run-ons

> ▶ A **sentence fragment** is an incomplete thought.
>
>   **Fragment:** Is the largest country in the world.
>   **Sentence:** The Soviet Union is the largest country in the world.
>
> ▶ A **run-on sentence** strings together too many thoughts without correct punctuation.
>
>   **Run-on:** It has a harsh climate, many problems arise.
>   **Simple Sentences:** It has a harsh climate. Many problems arise.
>   **Compound Sentence:** It has a harsh climate, **and** many problems arise.
>   **Complex Sentence: Because** it has a harsh climate, many problems arise.

Correct these sentence fragments and run-on sentences.

Example: Has a huge coastline.   **The Soviet Union has a huge coastline.**

1. In the Soviet Union, cold weather.
   _____

2. The country has a long coastline, most ports are used only in warm weather.
   _____

3. Inland waterways are also a problem, many freeze in winter.
   _____

4. Because of bad weather, many products.
   _____

5. Although travel by water would be cheaper.
   _____

6. The country has large deposits of coal and iron, it exports steel and machinery.
   _____

7. Many Soviet citizens are farmers, they grow wheat, rye, and corn.
   _____

8. Moscow and Leningrad the largest cities.
   _____

Level 8   Unit 1   The Sentence   (Use with pupil book pages 31–33.)
Skill: Students will correct sentence fragments and run-ons.

Name _____

RETEACHING WORKBOOK 10

LANGUAGE AND USAGE

10 Interjections

> ▶ An **interjection** shows strong feeling or represents a sound. Use a comma or an exclamation point after an interjection.

Common Interjections					
oh, dear	ah	hooray	well	oh, my	phew
oh, yes/no	aha	ouch	wow	ugh	shh

Wow! This is a bird watcher's paradise!
Oh, yes, there are over two hundred kinds of birds here.

Write each interjection and the punctuation mark that follows it.

Example: Oh, I like being at Yosemite National Park. _____ **Oh,** _____

1. Shh! I think I see a deer. _____

2. Goodness, it looks like a whole family. _____

3. Well, try not to frighten them, so I can take a picture. _____

4. Uh oh, they are starting to run away. _____

5. Phew! I managed to get the shot. _____

6. Hooray! You're the best photographer! _____

7. Hey, let's hike to Sentinel Falls today. _____

8. Okay, I ought to get some good pictures there. _____

9. Oh, my! Do the falls really drop two thousand feet? _____

10. Wow! That is quite a plunge! _____

11. Good grief, I've no more film for the camera. _____

12. Ugh! What do we do now? _____

13. Aha, there's a drugstore over there. _____

14. Oh, yes, I'm sure that they sell all kinds of film. _____

15. Bravo! We'll have great pictures after all! _____

Level 8 Unit 1 **The Sentence** *(Use with pupil book pages 34–35.)*
Skill: Students will identify interjections.

Houghton Mifflin English 8
Copyright © Houghton Mifflin Company. All rights reserved.

Name _____

RETEACHING WORKBOOK 11

COMPOSITION SKILL: PERSONAL NARRATIVE

Writing a Good Beginning

> Write a good beginning that will capture your readers' interest and will make them want to read on.
>
> **Poor Beginning:** Someone told me to stop as I walked in the door.
> **Good Beginning:** ''Halt!'' the security guard ordered, as alarms went off all around me.

Each personal narrative below needs a better beginning. Read the story. Then write a good beginning to replace the underlined sentence. Begin with an action, with dialogue, with details about the setting, or with details about yourself or another character.

The man told me that he needed help. I could see that he was breathing normally, so it was safe to leave him for a minute. I ran to a pay phone and called the emergency number. Then I rushed back to the man and introduced myself. I talked soothingly to him and tried to keep him calm. Within minutes we heard the sirens of an ambulance.

''Thank you, Gina,'' the injured man said as they carried him into the ambulance. ''You may have saved my life.''

Good Beginning: _____

_____

_____

_____

When I looked out the window the morning after the big snowstorm, there was a lot of snow. ''People are going to need some help digging out of this,'' I said to my little brother Don. ''Grab a shovel and let's go.''

School was canceled for the day, but many of our neighbors still had to get to work. We were able to dig out five driveways before breakfast. By then we'd worked up a huge appetite and earned ourselves more money than Don had ever made before. His eyes and cheeks were glowing as he wolfed down his breakfast.

Good Beginning: _____

_____

_____

_____

Level 8 Unit 2 Personal Narrative *(Use with pupil book pages 67–68.)*
Skill: Students will write good beginnings for stories.

Houghton Mifflin English 8
Copyright © Houghton Mifflin Company. All rights reserved.

UNIT 2 PERSONAL NARRATIVE

Name _____

RETEACHING WORKBOOK 12

COMPOSITION SKILL: PERSONAL NARRATIVE

Supplying Details

Use details that show what a person, place, thing, or event is like.

Poor Detail: Everyone teased me when I bowled.
Good Detail: My friends groaned and shrieked when I rolled another gutter ball.

The following paragraph from a personal narrative is not very interesting. Rewrite each sentence from the paragraph, adding details to show exactly what the event was like.

I played my best game ever last night. I had trained hard for it. I started doing things right from the very beginning. Some people told me I was doing really well. I felt good afterward.

1. I played my best game ever last night.

   _____

   _____

2. I had trained hard for it.

   _____

   _____

3. I started doing things right from the very beginning.

   _____

   _____

4. Some people told me I was doing really well.

   _____

   _____

5. I felt good afterward.

   _____

   _____

Level 8 Unit 2 Personal Narrative   (Use with pupil book page 69.)
Skill: Students will rewrite each sentence of a paragraph, adding details that show what an event was like.

Name _____

COMPOSITION SKILL: PERSONAL NARRATIVE

RETEACHING WORKBOOK **13**

Writing Dialogue

> Use **dialogue** in a story to make the characters and action seem real.
>
> **Without Dialogue:** Harriet said that she had enjoyed the science-fiction movie.
> **With Dialogue:** "Wow! Those were the most incredible special effects I've ever seen in a science-fiction movie," Harriet said.

Imagine that each situation described below has happened to you. Write a few lines of dialogue that you could use for a personal narrative about the situation. Try to show the feelings and personality of each character in the way he or she speaks.

1. Mary whispered some encouraging words to me before I went on stage. I thanked her.

_____

_____

_____

_____

2. Our new neighbor invited me to see her dog. I tried to get out of it. She insisted.

_____

_____

_____

_____

3. Rodney told me he had saved enough money to buy a racing bicycle at last. I was jealous but tried not to show it. I could tell that he knew anyway.

_____

_____

_____

_____

Level 8 Unit 2 Personal Narrative *(Use with pupil book pages 70–71.)*
Skill: Students will write dialogue for different situations.

Name _____

RETEACHING WORKBOOK 14

COMPOSITION SKILL: PERSONAL NARRATIVE

Writing a Good Ending

> A good ending *shows* rather than *tells* what happened. It leaves the reader with a feeling that fits the mood of the story.
>
> **Poor Ending:** It turned out in the end that I won the award.
> **Good Ending:** As I jumped out of my chair and ran up to receive the Athlete of the Year award, I couldn't help grinning from ear to ear.

Read the following closing paragraphs for personal narratives. Then write a good ending to replace the underlined sentences in each paragraph. Show rather than tell what happened.

Finally, we packed our suitcases, checked out of the hotel, and took the bus to the airport. <u>That's how our vacation in Hawaii ended. We had had a really good time and were sad to leave.</u>

Good Ending: _____

_____

_____

_____

We were breathing more heavily with every step. "I don't know if I can get to the top," whispered Marge. "I can't go another step." <u>She was really glad when I told her she didn't have to because I saw the marker that said we were actually already at the peak.</u>

Good Ending: _____

_____

_____

_____

Level 8 Unit 2 Personal Narrative   (Use with pupil book pages 72–73.)
Skill: Students will write good endings for stories.

Name _____

RETEACHING WORKBOOK 15

THE WRITING PROCESS: PERSONAL NARRATIVE

Step 3: Revise

Have I	yes
written a new beginning that captures the reader's attention?	☐
crossed out dull parts and added details that *show* rather than *tell*?	☐
added dialogue that makes the characters seem real?	☐
written a new ending that fits the mood of the story and that *shows* rather than *tells*?	☐

Revise the following story. Use the check list above to help you. Check off each box when you have finished your revision.
● Use the space above each line, on the sides, and below the paragraphs for your changes.

I went to the mall on Saturday. I was riding up an escalator

when the front of my sandal got caught at the top of the moving

stairway. I looked down in amazement. I tugged at the shoe.

It wouldn't come loose. I didn't know what to do.

Meanwhile, the escalator was bringing a crowd of people

toward me. I stepped out of the way. There I stood, with one

shoe on. I watched the other shoe flop around as people passed

by it.

A crowd gathered around me, and many people offered

advice. Finally, a girl my age knocked the sandal loose.

Everyone cheered. It was embarrassing.

Level 8 Unit 2 Personal Narrative (Use with pupil book pages 77–78.)
Skill: Students will revise a story, improving the beginning and the ending, crossing out dull parts, and adding details and dialogue.

Houghton Mifflin English 8
Copyright © Houghton Mifflin Company. All rights reserved.

Name _____

RETEACHING WORKBOOK **16**

THE WRITING PROCESS: PERSONAL NARRATIVE

Step 4: Proofread

When you proofread, look for mistakes in spelling, capitalization, and punctuation. Use proofreading marks to make corrections.

the begining of september is always busy said Ed

Proofreading Marks				
⌐⊢ Indent. ∧ Add something.	⋏ Add a comma. ∿ Reverse the order.	⊙ Add a period. ℐ Take out.	≡ Capitalize. ／ Make a small letter.	Add quotation marks.

Proofread the following story. There are three spelling mistakes, two run-on sentences, two sentence fragments, four punctuation errors, and four capitalization errors. Correct the errors. Use a dictionary to check your spelling.

In the middle of the night, leo let out a realy loud yell "It's a bear!" he

shouted. "I can see its eyes shineing in the bushes."

Everyone came running from the tents, we all talked at once. "You must have

imagined it, Leo."

leo pointed his flashlight. Toward the bushes.

"Don't do that, or the Bear will come here," Stu said

"I thought you didn't believe me," Leo grinned.

We all looked at each other nobody said anything. Just in case, we silently

grabed our sleeping bags and moved. Into the log Cabin.

The next morning we found a big raccoon that was sound asleep right outside

the tents? "Is this your bear?" we asked Leo

Level 8 Unit 2 Personal Narrative   (Use with pupil book pages 79–80.)
Skill: Students will proofread a story, correcting mistakes in spelling, punctuation, and capitalization.

Name _____

RETEACHING WORKBOOK · **17**

LANGUAGE AND USAGE

1 | Kinds of Nouns

> ► A **common noun** names any person, place, thing, or idea.
> ► A **proper noun** names a particular person, place, thing, or idea.
> ► A **concrete noun** names something that can be touched or seen.
> ► An **abstract noun** names an idea, a feeling, or a quality.
>
> | **Common:** | doctor | zoo | river | document |
> | **Proper:** | Doctor Klea | Bronx Zoo | Hudson River | Bill of Rights |
>
> | **Concrete:** | library | Ohio River | Italians | referee | motorboats |
> | **Abstract:** | lateness | Arbor Day | liberty | publicity | puzzlement |

Write each noun. Label it *common* or *proper* and then *concrete* or *abstract*.

Example: The students were studying history.

      students—common, concrete   history—common, abstract

1. A huge fire once nearly destroyed Chicago.

   _____

2. The blaze lit up the sky like the Fourth of July.

   _____

   _____

3. The flames had a major effect on the future of this city.

   _____

   _____

4. The cause of this event has become a legend.

   _____

   _____

5. In a barn owned by the O'Learys, a cow kicked over a lantern.

   _____

   _____

6. Oddly enough, the O'Learys' cottage did not burn to the ground.

   _____

Level 8 Unit 3 Nouns   *(Use with pupil book pages 88–89.)*
Skill: Students will identify common, proper, concrete, and abstract nouns.

UNIT 3 NOUNS

Houghton Mifflin English 8
Copyright © Houghton Mifflin Company. All rights reserved.

Name _____

RETEACHING WORKBOOK **18**

LANGUAGE AND USAGE

2 | **Compound and Collective Nouns**

> ▶ A **compound noun** is made up of two or more words.
> ▶ A **collective noun** names a group of people, animals, or things.
>
> **Compound Nouns:** spaceport   self-control   space probe   Martin Luther King
> **Collective Nouns:** class   committee   flock   community

A. Write the compound noun in each sentence.

Example: A crowd gathered near the launch pad.   _____launch pad_____

1. Reaching outer space had always been one of our greatest dreams. _____

2. On July 20, 1969, the *Eagle,* a small spacecraft, landed on the moon. _____

3. Neil Armstrong became the first human to set foot upon the moon's surface. _____

4. Edwin E. Aldrin, Jr., his copilot, joined him. _____

5. The astronauts brought back close-ups of the moon's surface. _____

6. From liftoff to landing, it was a historic flight. _____

B. Write the collective noun in each sentence.

Example: A crowd of people applauded enthusiastically.   _____crowd_____

7. Everyone watched the members of the space crew appear. _____

8. A scout troop waved a ''Welcome Home'' banner. _____

9. A school band played the national anthem. _____

10. The public celebrated our country's first moon landing. _____

11. Our class watched on television. _____

12. All over the nation, many groups watched this event. _____

Level 8   Unit 3   Nouns   (*Use with pupil book pages 90–91.*)
Skill: Students will identify compound and collective nouns.

Name _____   **RETEACHING WORKBOOK**   **19**

LANGUAGE AND USAGE

3 | Singular and Plural Nouns

▶ To form the plural of most singular nouns, add *s*.
▶ To form the plural of nouns ending with *s, x, z, sh,* or *ch*, add *es*.
▶ Some nouns have special plural forms.

| **Singular Nouns:** | ant | bunch | belief | sky | life | woman | dues | series |
| **Plural Nouns:** | ant**s** | bunch**es** | belief**s** | sk**ies** | li**ves** | wom**en** | dues | series |

| **Singular Nouns:** | crisis | son-in-law | close-up | Macy | 6 | *and* |
| **Plural Nouns:** | cris**es** | son**s**-in-law | close-up**s** | Macy**s** | 6**'s** | *and***'s** |

Write the plural form of each noun. Use your dictionary if necessary.

Example: get-together **get-togethers**

1. sandwich _____   16. sister-in-law _____

2. McCoy _____   17. life _____

3. radio _____   18. piano _____

4. turkey _____   19. spoonful _____

5. buzz _____   20. deer _____

6. mouse _____   21. goose _____

7. tongs _____   22. alumnus _____

8. & _____   23. cuff _____

9. great-uncle _____   24. family _____

10. editor in chief _____   25. potato _____

11. beach _____   26. box _____

12. guess _____   27. child _____

13. physics _____   28. dash _____

14. scissors _____   29. *but* _____

15. squeeze play _____   30. onion _____

Level 8 Unit 3 Nouns *(Use with pupil book pages 92–94.)*
Skill: Students will form plural nouns.

Name _____ RETEACHING WORKBOOK 20

LANGUAGE AND USAGE

4 | Possessive Nouns

> ▶ A **possessive noun** shows ownership.
> ▶ To form the possessive of a singular noun, a plural noun not ending with *s*, or a compound noun, add an apostrophe and *s*.
> ▶ To form the possessive of a plural noun ending with *s*, add an apostrophe only.
>
> | **Singular Possessive Nouns** | **Plural Possessive Nouns** |
> |---|---|
> | my **nephew's** birthday | our **ponies'** stable |
> | the **head of state's** office | **daughters-in-law's** relatives |
> | **Andrew Cass's** wedding | the **children's** teacher |
> | **Eve's** and **Keisha's** houses | **Eve and Keisha's** house |

Write the correct possessive nouns to complete these phrases.

Example: the coats of the guests   the ____guests'____ coats

1. the office of the lawyers   the _____ office
2. the jobs that my sisters-in-law have   my _____ jobs
3. the jeep belonging to the driver   the _____ jeep
4. money that Dan and Jay each have   _____ and _____ money
5. the suit worn by Tess   _____ suit
6. the pens that the editors in chief own   the _____ pens
7. the hat that belongs to the sheriff   the _____ hat
8. the food that the grandmothers made   the _____ food
9. a dog that my aunt and uncle both own   my _____ and _____ dog
10. the feathers of the turkeys   the _____ feathers
11. the antlers these deer have   these _____ antlers
12. the picture belonging to the Scotts   the _____ picture
13. the computer owned by John Celi   _____ computer
14. the movie the actress made   the _____ movie
15. a cat that Lee and Art own together   _____ and _____ cat

Level 8 Unit 3 Nouns   (Use with pupil book pages 95–96.)
Skill: Students will form singular and plural possessive nouns.

Name _____

RETEACHING WORKBOOK **21**

LANGUAGE AND USAGE

5 | Combining Sentences: Appositives

- ▶ An **appositive** is a noun or a phrase that identifies another noun.
- ▶ Use commas to set off an appositive that is not needed to complete the meaning of a sentence.

St. Augustine is on the coast of Florida.
St. Augustine is the oldest city in the nation.
                    appositive
St. Augustine, **the oldest city in the nation,** is on the coast of Florida.

Combine each pair of sentences by changing the underlined words into an appositive. Use commas where they are needed.

Example: St. Augustine attracts many tourists. It is a historical city in Florida.

St. Augustine, a historical city in Florida, attracts many tourists.

1. The earliest settlement in the United States was founded in 1565.
   The settlement in the United States was St. Augustine.

   _____

2. The city's central fortress was built by the Spanish people in the 1600s. The fortress was Castillo de San Marcos.

   _____

3. It overlooks Matanzas Bay. The bay is the entrance to St. Augustine.

   _____

4. The fort's main purpose made this an ideal location.
   The purpose was the protection of Spanish ships.

   _____

5. The British explorer tried to capture St. Augustine.
   The British explorer was Sir Francis Drake.

   _____

6. The battles over the city ended when the United States bought Florida from Spain. The city was a strategic spot.

   _____

Level 8 Unit 3 Nouns *(Use with pupil book pages 97–99.)*
Skill: Students will combine sentences, using appositives.

Houghton Mifflin English 8
Copyright © Houghton Mifflin Company. All rights reserved.

Name _____   **RETEACHING WORKBOOK** **23**

COMPOSITION SKILL: COMPARISON AND CONTRAST

Main Idea and Supporting Details

A **paragraph** is a group of sentences that has one main idea. All the sentences in the paragraph must support the main idea.

Read each of the following paragraphs. Write the main idea of each one. Draw a line through any sentence that does not support the main idea.

A.   When I received a Great Dane puppy as a birthday present, I got a big surprise. I had always wanted a nice little pet, but Topaz was growing by the minute. Topaz was not only large, but she was strong as well. Usually I end up being dragged on one of our walks. Topaz came from a litter of eight puppies.

Main Idea: _____

_____

_____

B.   Now that I have Topaz, I have realized how many responsibilities there are in owning a dog. Dogs need shots, regular exercise, and attention. You have to teach dogs how to heel, come when called, and sit upon command. I do not like walking Topaz in the rain. Topaz's funny habits keep the whole family laughing.

Main Idea: _____

_____

_____

C.   Many people agree that the North American spoon weevil is one of the least harmful insects. Their conclusion is based on several facts. In the first place, the spoon weevil never destroys crops or property. Secondly, it never stings or bites people or animals. Finally, it never makes too much noise. The insects are named after their favorite recreational facility—the spoon.

Main Idea: _____

_____

_____

Level 8 Unit 4 **Comparison and Contrast**   *(Use with pupil book pages 127–128.)*
Skill: Students will identify the main ideas in paragraphs and will identify sentences that do not support the main ideas.

Name _____

RETEACHING WORKBOOK   **24**

COMPOSITION SKILL: COMPARISON AND CONTRAST

Topic Sentences

> The **topic sentence** states the main idea of the paragraph. A good topic sentence states the main idea clearly and uses lively, exact language.

Each of the following paragraphs needs a better topic sentence. Read each paragraph and decide what the main idea is. Then write two good topic sentences to replace the underlined one. Put a check next to the topic sentence you like better.

A.   I have seen some animals in the mountains. Early in the morning, while the sky is still gray, birds sing outside the windows of our cabin on the mountain. During the morning jays and sparrows flit in the sun. Yellow butterflies land on the flowers and tree branches. In the afternoon chipmunks scurry through the bushes. Rabbits dart across the clearing. At night raccoons scavenge for food from our garbage pails.

Topic Sentence: _____

_____

_____

Topic Sentence: _____

_____

_____

B.   Gilbert Stuart was an artist of the 1700s. George Washington was one of his famous subjects. Stuart painted three different portraits of George Washington between 1795 and 1796. Of the three portraits, none is more familiar than the one that appears on the dollar bill. Almost everyone knows whose face is on the bill, but few people know the identity of the artist who painted it.

Topic Sentence: _____

_____

_____

Topic Sentence: _____

_____

_____

Level 8   Unit 4   Comparison and Contrast   *(Use with pupil book pages 128–129.)*
Skill: Students will write two topic sentences for paragraphs and will choose the topic sentence in each pair they prefer.

Name _____

RETEACHING WORKBOOK **25**

COMPOSITION SKILL: COMPARISON AND CONTRAST

Organizing Comparison and Contrast Paragraphs

When you **compare** two things, explain how they are alike. When you **contrast** two things, explain how they are different.

Read the following pairs of topics for comparison and contrast paragraphs. Then choose one pair and follow the directions below.

field hockey and ice hockey	city living and country living
movies and stage plays	travel by car and by train

A. List two ways in which the two items you chose are alike. Then write a topic sentence that you could use for a paragraph comparing the two items.

Similarities:

1. _____

_____

2. _____

_____

Topic Sentence for Comparison Paragraph: _____

_____

B. Now list two differences between the two items in your topic. Then write a topic sentence that you could use for a paragraph contrasting the two items.

Differences:

1. _____

_____

2. _____

_____

Topic Sentence for Contrast Paragraph: _____

_____

_____

Level 8 Unit 4 **Comparison and Contrast** *(Use with pupil book pages 130–131.)*
Skill: Students will list similarities and differences between two items and will write topic sentences for comparison and contrast paragraphs about the two items.

Houghton Mifflin English 8
Copyright © Houghton Mifflin Company. All rights reserved.

Name _____

RETEACHING WORKBOOK 26

THE WRITING PROCESS: COMPARISON AND CONTRAST

Step 3: Revise

Have I	yes
included a topic sentence that states the main idea clearly?	☐
crossed out any sentences that do not belong?	☐
added examples and details to make the comparison clearer?	☐
replaced vague, fuzzy language with more exact words to make the meaning clear?	☐

Revise the following paragraph of comparison. Use the check list above to help you. Check off each box when you have finished your revision.
- Use a thesaurus to help find exact words.
- Use the space above each line, on the sides, and below the paragraph for your changes.

Both of my friends like movies, for instance. Natalie likes

comedies, though, while Becky likes adventure stories. Becky

likes outdoor games. Becky and I spend hours talking about the

stuff that is bothering us. Natalie and I can talk for hours. Becky

almost always has something helpful to say about how maybe I

could go about solving a problem. So does Natalie. Becky is

really friendly and outgoing. Natalie tends to be quieter and have

just a few friends. They're both really likable, though. I'm glad

they're my friends!

Level 8 Unit 4 Comparison and Contrast *(Use with pupil book pages 135–136.)*
Skill: Students will revise a comparison paragraph, adding a topic sentence, crossing out any sentences that do not belong, and adding details and exact nouns.

Name _____

RETEACHING WORKBOOK 27

THE WRITING PROCESS: COMPARISON AND CONTRAST

Step 4: Proofread

> When you proofread, look for mistakes in spelling, punctuation, and capitalization. Use proofreading marks to correct the mistakes.
>
> One sister Elizabeth has many ~~hobby~~ *hobbies*.

Proofreading Marks

⌐ Indent.	⅄ Add a comma.	⊙ Add a period.	≡ Capitalize.	Add quotation marks.
∧ Add something.	∽ Reverse the order.	℘ Take out.	/ Make a small letter.	

A. Proofread the following paragraph. There are two missing punctuation marks and two mistakes in capitalization. There are two spelling mistakes and one run-on sentence. Find these mistakes and correct them. Use a dictionary to check your spelling.

  Two types of reptiles alligators and crocodiles have many things in common. Both are large animals that live in rivers and swamps in tropical areas. The female Alligator lays its eggs near the water. It guards its nest and its babys carefully similarly, the female Crocodile's nest is also along the shoreline. Noone should try to get near either animal's nest.

B. Proofread the following paragraph. There is one run-on sentence, one capitalization error, two spelling errors, and two incorrect possessive nouns. Find and correct the errors.

  In some ways, however, Alligators and crocodiles are very different in their appearance and activitys. The crocodiles head is narrow and pointed the alligators' head, on the oter hand, is broad and rounded. Alligators are very noisy animals, but crocodiles tend to be quieter.

Level 8   Unit 4   Comparison and Contrast   *(Use with pupil book pages 137–138.)*
Skill: Students will proofread paragraphs, correcting mistakes in spelling, capitalization, punctuation, and grammar.

Houghton Mifflin English 8
Copyright © Houghton Mifflin Company. All rights reserved.

Name _____ **RETEACHING WORKBOOK** 29

LANGUAGE AND USAGE

1 | Kinds of Verbs

> ▶ A **verb** expresses physical action, mental action, or being.
> ▶ A **linking verb** expresses being. It links the subject with a word in the predicate that describes or identifies the subject.
>
> **Action Verbs:** Farmers **use** natural resources.
> They **grow** much of the world's food.
> They **want** successful harvests.
>
> **Being Verbs:** There **are** many different types of farms.
> Farming **remains** an important occupation. *(linking verb)*
> Farmers **grow** very strong from their work. *(linking verb)*

A. Write each underlined verb. Label it *action* or *being*.

Example: That farm on the hillside <u>looks</u> beautiful. _____ looks—being

1. We <u>visited</u> a farm last week. _____

2. A friend of mine <u>works</u> there. _____

3. Work on a farm <u>seems</u> difficult. _____

4. There <u>are</u> different chores for every season. _____

5. Farmers <u>rise</u> early in the morning. _____

6. Their schedule <u>sounds</u> exhausting. _____

7. For many farmers the hard work <u>is</u> worthwhile. _____

8. They <u>enjoy</u> their independence. _____

B. Write each underlined verb. Label it *action* or *linking*.

Example: We <u>tasted</u> the newly picked beans. _____ tasted—action

9. Farmers <u>grow</u> accustomed to weather changes. _____

10. At times storms <u>appear</u> without warning. _____

11. Farmers <u>look</u> for signs of weather patterns. _____

12. Their crops <u>grow</u> best in certain conditions. _____

13. Plants <u>look</u> healthier after a good season. _____

14. They <u>taste</u> better as well. _____

Level 8 Unit 5 Verbs   *(Use with pupil book pages 146–147.)*
Skill: Students will identify action and linking verbs.

Name _____ **RETEACHING WORKBOOK** **30**

LANGUAGE AND USAGE

2 | Verb Phrases

> ▸ A **verb phrase** includes a main verb and one or more helping verbs.
> ▸ The **main verb** expresses the action or being.
> ▸ The **helping verb** or verbs help complete the meaning of the main verb.

Helping Verbs	Main Verbs
William Penn **had**	**proposed** plans for Philadelphia in 1682.
I'**m**	**visiting** the city today.
We **did**n't	**see** the Liberty Bell on our last trip.
Have you ever	**been** to Philadelphia?

Write the verb phrase in each sentence.

Example: Philadelphia is located on the Delaware River. _____ **is located** _____

1. Do you remember William Penn from your study of American history?

   _____

2. Penn had always dreamed of a ''city of brotherly love.''

   _____

3. Philadelphia could have been the nation's capital.

   _____

4. Philadelphia did become an important city in colonial America.

   _____

5. Would you have enjoyed Philadelphia in the 1600s?

   _____

6. I just can't imagine it during the seventeenth century.

   _____

7. Benjamin Franklin was living in Philadelphia in 1723.

   _____

8. He'd been looking for work in the large city.

   _____

Level 8 Unit 5 **Verbs**   *(Use with pupil book pages 148–149.)*
Skill: Students will identify verb phrases.

Houghton Mifflin English 8
Copyright © Houghton Mifflin Company. All rights reserved.

Name _____

RETEACHING WORKBOOK **31**

LANGUAGE AND USAGE

3 | Tenses

▶ Every verb has four **principal parts**.
▶ Verbs have different **tenses** to express different times.
▶ Use the principal parts of a verb to form its tenses.

Verb	**Present Participle**	**Past**	**Past Participle**
walk	(is) walking	walked	(has) walked

Present Tense: I **carry** the flag.
Past Tense: I **carried** the flag.
Future Tense: I **will carry** the flag.

Present Perfect Tense: We **have stopped** for a rest.
Past Perfect Tense: We **had stopped** for a rest.
Future Perfect Tense: We **will have stopped** for a rest.

A. Write the three simple tense forms of each verb with *they*.

Example: work they __*work*__ they __*worked*__ they __*will work*__

1. open they _____ they _____ they _____

2. drop they _____ they _____ they _____

3. close they _____ they _____ they _____

4. marry they _____ they _____ they _____

B. Write each sentence, using the tense of the verb shown in parentheses.

Example: The city __?__ upon a plan for the park. (decide—present perfect)

The city has decided upon a plan for the park. _____

5. The concrete in the old pool __?__ . (crack—past perfect)

_____

6. Workers __?__ it by next summer. (fix—future perfect)

_____

7. A local store __?__ paint for the weathered picnic tables. (supply—past)

_____

8. Volunteers __?__ a day for the litter pickup. (plan—present perfect)

_____

Level 8 Unit 5 Verbs *(Use with pupil book pages 150–152.)*
Skill: Students will form the principal parts of verbs and will write simple and perfect tenses.

Houghton Mifflin English 8
Copyright © Houghton Mifflin Company. All rights reserved.

Name _____ RETEACHING WORKBOOK 32

LANGUAGE AND USAGE

4 | Forms of *be*, *have*, and *do*

- You can use *be*, *have*, and *do* as main verbs and as helping verbs.
- *Be*, *have*, and *do* have different forms for different subjects and for different tenses.

Subjects	Forms of *be*	Forms of *have*	Forms of *do*
I	am, was	have, had	do, did
he, she, it	is, was	has, had	does, did
singular nouns	is, was	has, had	does, did
we, you, they	are, were	have, had	do, did
plural nouns	are, were	have, had	do, did

Write the correct form of the verb in parentheses to complete each sentence.

Example: A zoo ___is___ a place with many animals. (is, are)

1. A large zoo _____ animals from all over the world. (has, have)
2. Most zoo animals _____ in cages. (is, are)
3. _____ some animals live in open areas? (Doesn't, Don't)
4. Why _____ people visit zoos? (does, do)
5. We _____ fascinated by the way animals look and behave. (is, are)
6. Zoos _____ only provide entertainment. (doesn't, don't)
7. They _____ also laboratories for zoologists. (is, are)
8. What _____ a zoologist do? (does, do)
9. Zoology _____ the study of animals. (is, are)
10. The first known zoo _____ in Egypt in about 1500 B.C. (was, were)
11. An Egyptian queen _____ a collection of animals. (have, had)
12. _____ it attract great interest? (Does, Do)
13. Many zoos _____ beautiful gardens. (has, have)
14. The word *zoo* _____ short for "zoological garden." (is, are)
15. _____ you at the zoo last week? (Was, Were)
16. I _____ visiting our zoo on Tuesday. (am, are)

Level 8 Unit 5 Verbs (Use with pupil book pages 153–154.)
Skill: Students will choose forms of *be*, *have*, and *do* to agree with singular and plural subjects.

Name _____   **RETEACHING WORKBOOK**   **33**

LANGUAGE AND USAGE

5 | Irregular Verbs

▶ **Irregular verbs** do not follow any rules for forming the past and the past participle. You must learn the principal parts of irregular verbs.

Verb	Present Participle	Past	Past Participle
be	(is) being	was, were	(has) been
have	(is) having	had	(has) had
do	(is) doing	did	(has) done
put	(is) putting	put	(has) put
run	(is) running	ran	(has) run
bring	(is) bringing	brought	(has) brought
make	(is) making	made	(has) made

A. Write the missing principal parts of the following irregular verbs.

		Present Participle	Past	Past Participle
Example:	have	(is) having	had	(has) had
1.	hold			
2.	hurt			
3.	find			
4.	leave			
5.	win			
6.	let			
7.	read			
8.	burst			
9.	set			
10.	catch			
11.	cost			
12.	come			
13.	think			

Houghton Mifflin English 8
Copyright © Houghton Mifflin Company. All rights reserved.

Level 8   Unit 5   Verbs   *(Use with pupil book pages 155–157.)*
Skill: Students will form the principal parts of irregular verbs.

Name _____

RETEACHING WORKBOOK 34

LANGUAGE AND USAGE

6 | More Irregular Verbs

▸ You must learn the principal parts of irregular verbs.

Verb	Present Participle	Past	Past Participle
begin	(is) beginning	began	(has) begun
ring	(is) ringing	rang	(has) rung
choose	(is) choosing	chose	(has) chosen
see	(is) seeing	saw	(has) seen

Write the missing principal parts of the following irregular verbs.

	Present Participle	Past	Past Participle
Example: sink	(is) sinking	sank	(has) sunk
1. break			
2. drive			
3. speak			
4. wear			
5. give			
6. forget			
7. drink			
8. lie			
9. swim			
10. grow			
11. sing			
12. freeze			
13. write			
14. eat			

Houghton Mifflin English 8
Copyright © Houghton Mifflin Company. All rights reserved.

Level 8   Unit 5   Verbs   *(Use with pupil book pages 158–159.)*
Skill: Students will form the principal parts of irregular verbs.

Name _____

RETEACHING WORKBOOK **35**

LANGUAGE AND USAGE

7 | Progressive Forms

> ▶ Each tense has a **progressive form** to express continuing action.
> ▶ Form the progressive with an appropriate tense of *be* plus the present participle.
>
> **Present Progressive:** The students **are rehearsing**.
> **Past Progressive:** They **were rehearsing** yesterday.
> **Future Progressive:** They **will be rehearsing** tomorrow.
> **Present Perfect Progressive:** They **have been rehearsing** all day.
> **Past Perfect Progressive:** They **had been rehearsing** earlier.
> **Future Perfect Progressive:** They **will have been rehearsing** for three hours by the end of the day.

Write the progressive verb form in each sentence.

Example: The director was taking attendance. _____**was taking**_____

1. The eighth grade students are preparing for a play next week. _____

2. They will be presenting *My Fair Lady*. _____

3. The music teacher has been working very hard with the actors. _____

4. The director had been holding rehearsals three days a week. _____

5. The cast is meeting every day after school. _____

6. The students were practicing their lines yesterday. _____

7. They will have been rehearsing for six weeks by the time of the performance. _____

8. They have been selling many tickets. _____

9. A large crowd will be attending the play. _____

10. Everyone is hoping for a big hit. _____

Level 8 Unit 5 Verbs *(Use with pupil book pages 160–161.)*
Skill: Students will identify progressive verb forms.

Name _____   **RETEACHING WORKBOOK** **36**

LANGUAGE AND USAGE

8 | Transitive and Intransitive Verbs

> ► A **transitive verb** expresses action that is directed toward a word in the predicate.
> ► The word to which the action is directed is the **object** of the verb.
> ► An **intransitive verb** does not have an object.
> ► Linking verbs are always intransitive.
>
> | **Transitive Verbs** | **Intransitive Verbs** |
> |---|---|
> | Viking explorers **named** Greenland. | Greenland **lies** in the North Atlantic. |
> | New lands **attracted** them. | Greenland **is** an island. |

Write each underlined verb. Label it *transitive* or *intransitive*.

Example: Sarah displayed a map of Greenland.   displayed—transitive

1. Greenland is the largest island in the world.   _____

2. An ice cap almost covers the island.   _____

3. Fifty-four thousand people live in Greenland.   _____

4. Many islanders fish for a living.   _____

5. Greenland has some farms.   _____

6. The farmers grow various crops.   _____

7. Some farmers on the island raise sheep.   _____

8. No forests exist in Greenland.   _____

9. Very few tourists ever visit Greenland.   _____

10. Some people see the ice cap from an airplane.   _____

11. The weather stays cold much of the year.   _____

12. Some people speak Greenlandic.   _____

13. Danish is also an official language.   _____

14. Most of Greenland lies within the Arctic Circle.   _____

15. Dog sleds carry Greenlanders over the snow.   _____

Level 8 Unit 5 Verbs   *(Use with pupil book pages 162–163.)*
Skill: Students will identify transitive and intransitive verbs.

Name _____

LANGUAGE AND USAGE

Direct and Indirect Objects

RETEACHING WORKBOOK — 37

> ► The **direct object** tells *who* or *what* receives the action of a transitive verb.
> ► The **indirect object** is a noun or a pronoun in the predicate that tells *to whom, for whom,* or *for what* the action is done.
>
>   direct   direct   direct
> Robots do many **jobs** and **chores**. They do **them** well.
>   indirect   direct   indirect direct
> Scientists give **robots commands**. They give **them orders** quickly.

Write each object. Then label it *direct* or *indirect*. The verbs are underlined to help you.

Example: Albert gave the robot a name.

            robot—indirect, name—direct

1. Many factories use special robots. _____

2. Engineers assign them tasks on assembly lines.

   _____

3. Robots can give cars a perfect paint job.

   _____

4. In households robots save people time and trouble.

   _____

5. Some robots wash dishes and floors. _____

6. They will do these things and other tasks with no complaint.

   _____

7. Robots occasionally disappoint their creators and owners.

   _____

8. The manufacturer sold Albert and me a defective robot.

   _____

Level 8   Unit 5 Verbs   *(Use with pupil book pages 164–166.)*
Skill: Students will identify direct and indirect objects.

Name _____

RETEACHING WORKBOOK **38**

LANGUAGE AND USAGE

10 | Predicate Nouns and Predicate Adjectives

> ▸ Predicate nouns and predicate adjectives follow linking verbs.
> ▸ A **predicate noun** identifies or renames the subject.
> ▸ A **predicate adjective** describes the subject.
>
> **Predicate Nouns:**   Keith is a hard **worker** and a good **friend**.
>
> **Predicate Adjective:** He looks **kind**.

Write the underlined words. Label them *predicate noun* or *predicate adjective*.

Example: The small radios are convenient.

   convenient—predicate adjective

1. Radios have been common items for many years.

   _____

2. Today stereo headsets seem almost equally popular.

   _____

3. Headsets have grown increasingly lightweight and sophisticated.

   _____

4. The items appeared harmless at first.

   _____

5. They were simply modern conveniences.

   _____

6. Recently, however, headsets have become a matter for concern.

   _____

7. Two possible hazards are accidents and ear damage.

   _____

8. Many health officials remain doubtful about the safety of headsets.

   _____

Houghton Mifflin English 8
Copyright © Houghton Mifflin Company. All rights reserved.

Level 8 Unit 5 Verbs   *(Use with pupil book pages 167–168.)*
Skill: Students will identify predicate nouns and predicate adjectives.

Name _____

RETEACHING WORKBOOK 39

LANGUAGE AND USAGE

11 | Active and Passive Voices

> ▸ A verb is in the **active voice** if the subject performs the action.
> ▸ A verb is in the **passive voice** if the subject receives the action.
> ▸ Use the passive voice when the doer of an action is unimportant.
> ▸ Use the active voice for direct, forceful sentences.
>
>   verb   direct object
> **Active Voice:** The dogs **found** the hikers.
>
>   subject   verb
> **Passive Voice:** The hikers **were found** by the dogs.

Underline the verb in each sentence. Then label the verb *active* or *passive*.

Example: Some dogs <u>search</u> for missing persons.   **active**

1. Rescue dogs are trained by special workers.   _____

2. The animals locate lost individuals.   _____

3. The dogs are given a scent from clothing.   _____

4. The clothing belongs to the missing person.   _____

5. Then the dogs follow the smell.   _____

6. Police use bloodhounds as search dogs.   _____

7. Criminals are found by the animals.   _____

8. Bloodhounds are used often in night searches.   _____

9. They have very poor eyesight.   _____

10. Therefore, bloodhounds rely on their sense of smell.   _____

11. Sometimes a scent can be masked by other odors.   _____

12. A scent is weakened by water or dampness.   _____

13. The dogs usually prove their value though.   _____

14. Some dogs have tracked people across rivers.   _____

15. Others have discovered people under snow.   _____

16. One person was found under fourteen feet of snow.   _____

Level 8   Unit 5   Verbs   (*Use with pupil book pages 169–170.*)
Skill: Students will identify active and passive verbs.

Houghton Mifflin English 8
Copyright © Houghton Mifflin Company. All rights reserved.

Name _____

RETEACHING WORKBOOK **40**

LANGUAGE AND USAGE

12 | **Subject-Verb Agreement**

> ▶ A subject and its verb must agree in number.
> ▶ Use a plural verb with a compound subject joined by *and.*
> ▶ Use a verb that agrees with the nearer of two subjects joined by *or* or *nor.*

Singular Subjects:	The geologist **studies** fossils.
	He **learns** about the past.
Plural Subjects:	Fossils **provide** clues about living things.
	They **require** careful study.
Compound Subjects:	Teachers and students **learn** from fossils.
	Either geologists or a student **collects** the fossils.
	Neither the technique nor the tools **are** perfect.

Write the verb in parentheses that agrees with the underlined subject.

Example: Scientists (collects, collect) fossils.   _collect_

1. A fossil (contain, contains) animal or plant remains. _____

2. Fossils (is, are) studied in many ways. _____

3. The scientist and her assistant (handle, handles) fossils carefully. _____

4. Either the scientist or her assistants (cleans, clean) the fossil. _____

5. Either chemicals or plain soap (is, are) used for cleaning. _____

6. Small hand tools and power tools also (helps, help). _____

7. The scientist (wants, want) to know the age of a fossil. _____

8. She (uses, use) an x-ray and radioactive dating methods. _____

9. Neither the x-ray nor radioactive dating methods (tells, tell)
the exact age of the fossil. _____

10. Instead they (provides, provide) approximate ages. _____

11. Scientists (learns, learn) a lot from this information. _____

12. It (tells, tell) about the history of the earth. _____

13. Neither the earth's landforms nor its wildlife (has, have) remained
the same. _____

14. A plant trace or animal fossils (records, record) the changes. _____

Level 8 Unit 5 Verbs *(Use with pupil book pages 171–172.)*
Skill: Students will choose verbs to agree with singular, plural, and compound subjects.

Houghton Mifflin English 8
Copyright © Houghton Mifflin Company. All rights reserved.

Name _____

RETEACHING WORKBOOK **41**

LANGUAGE AND USAGE

13 | More About Subject-Verb Agreement

> ▶ Use a singular verb with a title or a name of a single thing, with a collective noun referring to a whole group, and with a noun of amount.
> ▶ Use a plural verb with a collective noun referring to the individual members of a group and with a noun of amount when referring to the individual units.
>
> **Titles:** _Hard Times_ **is** a book by Charles Dickens.
> **Names:** Max and Weber **is** my favorite clothing store.
> **Nouns Ending with _s_:** Mathematics **is** challenging.
> The scissors **are** in the sewing box.
> **Collective Nouns:** The audience **claps** loudly.
> The audience **react** in different ways.
> **Nouns of Amounts:** Ten dollars **is** a lot of money.
> The ten dollars **were** set side by side.

Write the verb in parentheses that agrees with the underlined subject.

Example: The eighth grade class (is, are) having a party. _____**is**_____

1. Three weeks (is, are) enough time to plan a party. _____

2. News of the party (has, have) traveled fast. _____

3. Josie's Meatballs (is, are) catering the dinner. _____

4. Six dollars (seem, seems) like a fair price for a ticket. _____

5. The decoration crew (works, work) hard. _____

6. The group (is, are) all doing different jobs. _____

7. The art club (has, have) made a beautiful mural. _____

8. A string quartet (is, are) going to perform. _____

9. Actors Unlimited (is, are) performing a scene from a book. _____

10. _The Adventures of Tom Sawyer_ (is, are) the book. _____

11. The planning committee (has, have) suggested a dress code. _____

12. Denim pants (do, does) not suit the occasion. _____

13. Only three quarters (is, are) now left in the treasury. _____

14. Perhaps economics (is, are) not the class's best subject. _____

Level 8 Unit 5 Verbs _(Use with pupil book pages 173–175.)_
Skill: Students will choose verbs to agree with titles, names, collective nouns, nouns ending with _s_, and nouns of amount.

Houghton Mifflin English 8
Copyright © Houghton Mifflin Company. All rights reserved.

Name _____

RETEACHING WORKBOOK **42**

LANGUAGE AND USAGE

14 | Agreement in Inverted and Interrupted Order

▶ The subject of a sentence in **inverted** or **interrupted order** follows all or part of the predicate.
▶ First, find the subject. Then make the verb agree with it.

Inverted Order: On the news **are** maps of the weather.
There **are** two maps on the wall.
Have you ever **watched** the weather report?

Interrupted Order: The meteorologists on television **report** the weather.
Ms. Chu, one of the meteorologists, **predicts** the weather.

Write the verb in parentheses that agrees with each underlined subject.

Example: Maps on television (is, are) not true weather maps.   **are**

1. (Does, Do) most people understand a true weather map?   _____

2. Usually there (is, are) too much information for us.   _____

3. On the news programs (is, are) simpler maps.   _____

4. How (does, do) you forecast the weather?   _____

5. Changes in the weather (gives, give) important clues.   _____

6. The movement of air masses (tells, tell) meteorologists a lot.   _____

7. A ''low,'' one of the air-pressure centers, (signals, signal) oncoming storms.   _____

8. Why (is, are) the weather so hard to predict?   _____

9. There (is, are) so many factors to consider.   _____

10. Mark Twain, one of our most famous writers, (sums, sum) it up well.   _____

11. What (is, are) his famous remark about weather?   _____

12. In this book (is, are) the quotation.   _____

13. The quotation, one of Twain's witty sayings, (says, say) ''Everybody talks about the weather, but nobody does anything about it.''   _____

14. The control of weather conditions (remains, remain) beyond our abilities.   _____

Level 8 Unit 5 Verbs   *(Use with pupil book pages 176–177.)*
Skill: Students will choose verbs to agree with singular and plural subjects of sentences in inverted order and interrupted order.

Houghton Mifflin English 8
Copyright © Houghton Mifflin Company. All rights reserved.

Name _____   RETEACHING WORKBOOK 43

LANGUAGE AND USAGE

 lie, lay; rise, raise

> ▸ Use *lie* for "to rest or to remain." *Lie* is intransitive.
> ▸ Use *lay* for "to put or to place." *Lay* is transitive.
> ▸ Use *rise* for "to get up." *Rise* is intransitive.
> ▸ Use *raise* for "to lift or to grow." *Raise* is transitive.
>
>   direct object
>   Martha **will lie** down soon. She **will lay** her coat on the chair.
>   direct object
>   She **will rise** after a short nap. She **will raise** the shades.

Rewrite each sentence, using the correct verb form in parentheses.

Example: Martha (raises, rises) vegetables in her garden.
       Martha raises vegetables in her garden.

1. Martha (raised, rose) early this morning.

2. Everyone else in the family was still (lying, laying) in bed.

3. Martha had (lain, laid) her tools out the night before.

4. It is hard work to (raise, rise) vegetables.

5. Martha (raises, rises) carrots and onions.

6. She carefully (lay, laid) the seeds in the soil.

7. A quarter of an inch of soil (lay, laid) on top of them.

8. A few weeks later tiny seedlings (raised, rose) from the ground.

Level 8   Unit 5   Verbs   *(Use with pupil book page 178.)*
Skill: Students will use *lie, lay, rise,* and *raise* correctly.

Name _____

RETEACHING WORKBOOK **44**

LANGUAGE AND USAGE

16 | *affect, effect; accept, except*

> ▶ The verb *affect* means "to influence."
> ▶ The verb *effect* means "to cause to happen."
> ▶ The noun *effect* means "result."
> ▶ The verb *accept* means "to receive."
> ▶ The preposition *except* means "excluding."
>
> The new rules **will affect** everyone.
> The rules **should effect** many changes.
> Their **effect** will be felt quickly.
> The committee **accepted** most of the suggestions.
> The members agreed with all the ideas **except** one.

Rewrite each sentence, using the correct word in parentheses.

Example: The drought (affects, effects) three counties.

The drought affects three counties.

1. (Accept, Except) for last weekend, it has been a dry summer.

   _____

2. The weather has had a serious (affect, effect) on the local crops.

   _____

3. The lack of rain has (affected, effected) the reservoirs as well.

   _____

4. The water commission must (affect, effect) changes in water use.

   _____

5. Lin Lee has (accepted, excepted) a position on the Drought Emergency Team.

   _____

6. She has visited every town in the area (accept, except) Pine Bluff.

   _____

7. Most people are (accepting, excepting) the new water restrictions.

   _____

8. The only way to (affect, effect) change is for everyone to cooperate.

   _____

Level 8 Unit 5 Verbs   *(Use with pupil book page 179.)*
Skill: Students will use *affect, effect, accept,* and *except* correctly.

Houghton Mifflin English 8
Copyright © Houghton Mifflin Company. All rights reserved.

Name _____ **RETEACHING WORKBOOK** 45

COMPOSITION SKILL: STORY

Plot

> The **plot** of most stories follows this pattern: one or more characters have a problem, or **conflict**; the conflict builds to a **climax**; and the climax is followed by the **resolution**, or solution to the conflict.

Read the following plot summary. Then write one or two sentences, telling the conflict, the climax, and the resolution of the plot.

In one part of Mark Twain's *The Adventures of Tom Sawyer,* Tom finds that he has to whitewash, or paint, a fence along the sidewalk. It is a long, hard job, and he would like to get out of it. When some of his friends come by, Tom begins to give them a ''sales talk'' about what an important and demanding job whitewashing a fence is. Eventually, Tom does not have to paint the fence at all, because his friends have convinced themselves that it is something they really want to do. Tom concludes that work is something you have to do, while play is something you don't have to do.

Conflict: _____

_____

_____

_____

Climax: _____

_____

_____

_____

Resolution: _____

_____

_____

_____

Level 8   Unit 6   Story   *(Use with pupil book pages 214–215.)*
Skill: Students will identify the conflict, climax, and resolution of a story plot.

Name _____

RETEACHING WORKBOOK 46

COMPOSITION SKILL: STORY

Setting

> The particular place and time of a story are the **setting**. When you describe a setting, choose words and details that bring out a particular **mood**, or feeling surrounding the events.

Four settings in which a story might take place are listed below. List four words or details that create a mood of loneliness, mysteriousness, happiness, or excitement for each setting.

A. A small New England town

1. _____
2. _____
3. _____
4. _____

B. A camp in the Rocky Mountains

1. _____
2. _____
3. _____
4. _____

C. A country fair

1. _____
2. _____
3. _____
4. _____

D. A downtown street in a large city

1. _____
2. _____
3. _____
4. _____

Level 8 Unit 6 Story *(Use with pupil book pages 215–216.)*
Skill: Students will write details for four story settings, creating moods of loneliness, mysteriousness, happiness, or excitement.

Name _____

RETEACHING WORKBOOK **47**

COMPOSITION SKILL: STORY

Characters

> Any person or animal that takes part in the action of a story is a **character**. There are five main ways to show what a character is like. You can describe the character's personality and appearance. You can have the character speak or have another character speak about him or her. You can also show what the character does.

Imagine what each character below might be like. Then write one sentence to describe each character's appearance, personality or feelings, and actions.

A. A girl or boy six years of age

Appearance: _____

_____

Personality or Feelings: _____

_____

Actions: _____

B. A grandmother who owns her own business

Appearance: _____

_____

Personality or Feelings: _____

_____

Actions: _____

C. A bus driver or train conductor

Appearance: _____

_____

Personality or Feelings: _____

_____

Actions: _____

Houghton Mifflin English 8
Copyright © Houghton Mifflin Company. All rights reserved.

Level 8 Unit 6 Story *(Use with pupil book pages 217–218.)*
Skill: Students will show what characters are like by describing their appearance, personality or feelings, and actions.

Name _____

COMPOSITION SKILL: STORY

RETEACHING WORKBOOK 48

Point of View

> When you write a story, choose a **point of view** from which to tell it. A **limited point of view** tells what one character in the story thinks, feels, and sees. The story can be told in the **first person** *(I)* or the **third person** *(he* or *she).*
>
> An **omniscient**, or **all-knowing**, **point of view** tells what all the characters in a story think, feel, and see. A story with this point of view is usually told in the third person.

The following paragraph from a story is told from a limited point of view. Rewrite the story from the point of view of an all-knowing narrator who can tell what all the characters think, feel, and see. The first sentence is provided below.

   I was looking around the classroom nervously as the teacher passed out the tests. She didn't look worried at all. In fact, she looked as if she was in a good mood. I could see Lydia staring at something on the windowsill, but I couldn't tell what. She seemed relaxed. Looking back, I saw Paul, who was tapping his pencil.

Omniscient Point of View:

   Everyone in the classroom had different thoughts and feelings as the tests were

being passed out. _____

_____

_____

_____

_____

_____

_____

Level 8 Unit 6 Story   *(Use with pupil book pages 219–221.)*
Skill: Students will rewrite a paragraph from a story, changing the point of view from limited to omniscient.

Name _____

RETEACHING WORKBOOK **49**

THE WRITING PROCESS: STORY

Step 3: Revise

Have I	yes
made the beginning of the story more interesting?	☐
crossed out any sentences that do not keep to the same point of view?	☐
added details to make the setting clearer?	☐
added dialogue, details, and actions to show what the characters are like?	☐

Revise the following paragraphs that begin a story. Use the check list above to help you. Check off each box when you have finished your revision.
- Use the space above each line, on the sides, and below the paragraphs for your changes.

Mrs. Wharton was kind of an interesting person. She lived

alone in a nice old house in the country. Whenever I visited her,

I enjoyed looking at the beautiful scenery.

The last time I saw her, she came out of her house and said

hello as I got out of my car. I'm so glad to see him, she

thought. I wondered why she looked so worried. I followed her

into her house, which looked the same as always. She told me

how nice I looked in my new clothes and then asked about my

family. I thanked her and said they were fine. Then I asked how

she was. She didn't answer. Instead, she told me why she had

asked me to come.

Houghton Mifflin English 8
Copyright © Houghton Mifflin Company. All rights reserved.

Level 8 Unit 6 Story *(Use with pupil book pages 225–226.)*
Skill: Students will revise the beginning of a story, making the beginning more interesting, deleting sentences that do not support the point of view, and adding details, dialogue, and actions.

Name _____

RETEACHING WORKBOOK **50**

THE WRITING PROCESS: STORY

Step 4: Proofread

> When you proofread, look for mistakes in spelling, capitalization, punctuation, and grammar. Use proofreading marks to make corrections.
>
> Tom asked for tomatos from ̶y̶our garden.

Proofreading Marks				
⌐ Indent.	⩔ Add a comma.	⊙ Add a period.	≡ Capitalize.	Add quotation marks.
∧ Add something.	∼ Reverse the order.	℘ Take out.	/ Make a small letter.	

A. Proofread the following paragraphs. There are two spelling errors, one capitalization error, one wrong punctuation mark, one mistake in paragraph format, and two verbs in the wrong tense. Correct the errors. Use a dictionary to check your spelling.

Bryan was excited about the race the next day. At dinner his sister tammy had

news that upset him,

She past him the potatos and then says, "I saw Sam Fox today. He wasn't

limping." "Oh, no!" groans Bryan. "That means he's going to run after all."

B. Proofread the following paragraphs from the same story. There are two spelling errors, one capitalization error, one wrong punctuation mark, and one missing punctuation mark. There are also one mistake in paragraph format and one subject-verb agreement error. Correct the errors.

"Don't let it upset you, Bryan," said his Father? "Didn't you just beat your

best time buy a minute? Remember all that training!"

"Yes, Dad, but I still think that I don't have a chance," Bryan replied, shaking

his head. Tammy chimed in, "Maybe there is other good runners but I can already

hear the echos of our cheers as you cross the finish line."

Level 8 Unit 6 Story *(Use with pupil book pages 227–228.)*
Skill: Students will proofread paragraphs of a story, correcting mistakes in spelling, punctuation, capitalization, and grammar.

Name _____

RETEACHING WORKBOOK **51**

LANGUAGE AND USAGE

1 | **Adjectives**

> ▶ An **adjective** describes, or modifies, a noun or a pronoun.
> ▶ A **proper adjective** is formed from a proper noun.
> ▶ *A, an,* and *the* are special adjectives called **articles**.
> ▶ A **predicate adjective** follows a linking verb and describes the subject.
>
> **Outerville's rebuilt** theater reopened **last** week.
> It looked **quaint** and **inviting**.
> **A local** playwright wrote **a new** play for **that** occasion.

Write each word used as an adjective. Include the articles *a, an,* and *the.*

Example: The talkative audience entered the quiet theater.

The, talkative, the, quiet
_____

1. A burgundy velvet curtain rose slowly on the lighted stage.

   _____

2. Three actors walked onto the set of an ordinary town.

   _____

3. One actor seemed quiet but cheerful. _____

4. The fascinating story took place in an Iowa town.

   _____

5. The actors' costumes were colorful. _____

6. A bright, young Asian designer had created ten elegant costumes.

   _____

7. The designer's work added a special touch to this amusing play.

   _____

8. At the end of the play, twenty pleased players took their bows.

   _____

9. The enchanted audience, smiling and appreciative, applauded the actors.

   _____

Level 8 Unit 7 Modifiers *(Use with pupil book pages 236–238.)*
Skill: Students will identify words used as adjectives.

Name _____

RETEACHING WORKBOOK **52**

LANGUAGE AND USAGE

2 | Comparing with Adjectives

> ▶ The **positive degree** is the basic form of the adjective.
> ▶ Use the **comparative degree** to compare two things.
> ▶ Use the **superlative degree** to compare three or more things.
> ▶ Form the comparative degree with -*er* or *more*.
> ▶ Form the superlative degree with -*est* or *most*.

Positive Degree	Comparative Degree	Superlative Degree
dirty	dirtier	dirtiest
bad	worse	worst
enjoyable	more enjoyable	most enjoyable

Rewrite each sentence, choosing the correct form of the adjective in parentheses.

Example: The Roeblings built the (more famous, most famous) bridge in New York City.

The Roeblings built the most famous bridge in New York City.

1. When it was completed, the Brooklyn Bridge was the (larger, largest) suspension bridge ever built.

_____

2. Its cables were the (longer, longest) ever used on a suspension bridge.

_____

3. In 1883 this bridge received (more, most) acclaim than any other bridge.

_____

4. The Brooklyn Bridge is (prettier, prettiest) than many other bridges.

_____

5. Bridges built earlier took (less, fewer) time to construct.

_____

6. Of all their creations, the Brooklyn Bridge was the Roeblings' (more impressive, most impressive).

_____

Level 8 Unit 7 Modifiers *(Use with pupil book pages 239–241.)*
Skill: Students will use the comparative and the superlative forms of adjectives.

Houghton Mifflin English 8
Copyright © Houghton Mifflin Company. All rights reserved.

Name _____

RETEACHING WORKBOOK **53**

LANGUAGE AND USAGE

3 | **Adverbs**

> ► An **adverb** modifies a verb, an adjective, or another adverb.
> ► An adverb tells *how, when, where,* or *to what extent.*
> ► **Intensifiers** are adverbs that tell *to what extent.*
>
> **How:** The class listened **carefully** to *Gulliver's Travels.*
> **When:** Our teacher **frequently** reads to us from this book.
> **Where:** We stayed **indoors** until the end of the chapter.
> **To What Extent:** The book is **quite** popular with the class.

Write each adverb. Then write the word or words that it modifies.

Example: Jonathan Swift sometimes wrote science fiction.

<u>**sometimes—wrote**</u>

1. Jonathan Swift wrote quite cleverly about a man named Gulliver.

   _____

2. Gulliver traveled first to a land of extremely small people.

   _____

3. Why did he go there?

   _____

4. Actually his ship had sunk nearby.

   _____

5. How did Gulliver communicate with these terribly frightened people?

   _____

6. Very quickly Gulliver showed his good intentions.

   _____

7. The giant Gulliver soon became rather useful to the tiny people.

   _____

8. Later Gulliver had other equally strange adventures.

   _____

Level 8 Unit 7 Modifiers *(Use with pupil book pages 242–244.)*
Skill: Students will identify adverbs and the words that they modify.

Houghton Mifflin English 8
Copyright © Houghton Mifflin Company. All rights reserved.

Name _____

LANGUAGE AND USAGE

4 Comparing with Adverbs

RETEACHING WORKBOOK

- The **positive degree** of an adverb describes one action.
- Use the **comparative degree** to compare two actions.
- Use the **superlative degree** to compare three or more actions.
- Form the comparative degree with *-er* or *more*.
- Form the superlative degree with *-est* or *most*.

Positive Degree	Comparative Degree	Superlative Degree
early	earlier	earliest
steadily	more steadily	most steadily
well	better	best

Rewrite each sentence, choosing the correct adverb in parentheses.

Example: The Mt. Baldy hike thrills us (more, most) every year.
The Mt. Baldy hike thrills us more every year.

1. Of all our hikes, the Mt. Baldy hike went (more smoothly, most smoothly).
   _____

2. Samina prepared for the hike (better, best) than any other hiker.
   _____

3. We started (earlier, earliest) in the morning than we did last year.
   _____

4. We also walked (farther, further) than we did last year.
   _____

5. Of all the climbers, Ramon walked (fastest, most fastest).
   _____

6. We climbed Mt. Baldy (more quickly, most quickly) than we did before.
   _____

7. With my sturdy boots, I climbed (more easily, most easily) than Dana.
   _____

8. Of all the hikers, Dana slowed down (less, least) near the top.
   _____

Level 8 Unit 7 Modifiers (Use with pupil book pages 245–247.)
Skill: Students will use the comparative and the superlative forms of adverbs.

Name _____   **RETEACHING** **55**
                                                              WORKBOOK

LANGUAGE AND USAGE

5 | Negatives

> ► A **negative** is a word or a contraction that means "no" or "not."
> ► A **double negative** is the incorrect use of two negatives to express one
>   negative idea. Avoid double negatives.
>
>   **Double Negative:** The moon does**n't** give off **no** light of its own.
>   **Correct:** The moon does**n't** give off any light of its own.
>   **Correct:** The moon gives off **no** light of its own.

Rewrite each sentence, choosing the correct word or words in parentheses.

Example: The moon isn't (anything, nothing) like the earth.

   The moon isn't anything like the earth.

1. The moon (is, isn't) hardly as large as the earth.

    _____

2. Rain doesn't (never, ever) fall on the moon.

    _____

3. The moon (has, hasn't) neither an atmosphere nor weather.

    _____

4. Not (anything, nothing) on the moon weighs the same as it does on earth.

    _____

5. I don't believe (any, no) old tales about the moon.

    _____

6. No cow (never, ever) jumped over the moon.

    _____

7. There isn't (no, any) green cheese on the moon.

    _____

8. The moon does not follow (nobody, anybody).

    _____

Level 8   Unit 7   **Modifiers**   *(Use with pupil book pages 248–249.)*
Skill: Students will use negatives correctly.

Name _____

LANGUAGE AND USAGE

RETEACHING WORKBOOK 56

  Adjective or Adverb?

> ▶ Use *good*, *bad*, *sure*, and *real* as adjectives.
> ▶ Use *well*, *badly*, *surely*, and *really* as adverbs.
> ▶ Use *well* as an adjective only when it refers to health.
>
> **Adjectives**
> The scientist's ideas were **good**.
> She wasn't **sure** about every invention.
> Today her stomach didn't feel **well**.
>
> **Adverbs**
> She studied her notes **well**.
> One formula **surely** puzzled her.
> An experiment went **badly**.

Rewrite each sentence, choosing the correct adjective or adverb in parentheses.

Example: (Sure, Surely) you've heard about Dr. Strangely's experiments.
Surely you've heard about Dr. Strangely's experiments.

1. Dr. Strangely was a (real, really) amazing scientist.

   _____

2. This clever scientist (sure, surely) created many new inventions.

   _____

3. Her inventions weren't (bad, badly); they were different.

   _____

4. She invented a method of helping people think (good, well).

   _____

5. Her intentions were always (good, well).

   _____

6. One invention was for baseball pitchers who had been pitching (bad, badly).

   _____

7. She hoped that one of her formulas would help sick people feel (good, well).

   _____

8. (Real, Really) quickly, she gained many appreciative customers.

   _____

Level 8   Unit 7   Modifiers   (Use with pupil book pages 250–251.)
Skill: Students will distinguish between adjectives and adverbs.

Name _____ **RETEACHING WORKBOOK** **57**

COMPOSITION SKILL: DESCRIPTION

Choosing Details

> When you write a description, choose details that suit your purpose and your **point of view,** or attitude.

Read each of these situations. Follow the directions.

A. Here is the way a classified advertisement might describe a dog for sale:

two-year-old golden retriever, female, gentle: $40

If you call the dog's owners, they will probably tell you more details that they hope will make you want to buy the dog. List four details that would tell you more about the dog and would make you feel you want to buy it.

1. _____

2. _____

3. _____

4. _____

B. You are writing a letter to your cousins in a distant city, asking them to entertain a friend who will be visiting there. List four details so that your cousins will recognize your friend and be glad to meet him or her.

5. _____

6. _____

7. _____

8. _____

C. You have gone away to camp for two weeks and are not having a good time. In a letter to a friend, you tell about things that you don't like. List four details you might include in your letter.

9. _____

10. _____

11. _____

12. _____

Level 8 Unit 8 Description   *(Use with pupil book pages 282–284.)*
Skill: Students will write details about people, places, and things that create particular impressions.

Name _____

RETEACHING WORKBOOK **58**

COMPOSITION SKILL: DESCRIPTION

Using Descriptive Language

Use exact adjectives, nouns, verbs, and adverbs, as well as **similes** and **metaphors**, to create vivid pictures in your reader's mind.

Exact Words: The athlete leaps aggressively for rebounds.
Simile: The athlete is *like a tightly coiled spring* on the court.
Metaphor: The athlete *is a tiger* when she leaps for rebounds.

Rewrite each sentence, replacing the underlined word or words with more exact words. Use at least one simile and at least one metaphor.

1. The pretty building was on a nice beach.

   _____

   _____

2. Marty looked tired.

   _____

3. Jack has a nice smile.

   _____

4. The city lights look wonderful from the top of that skyscraper.

   _____

   _____

5. We saw a person go down that slide.

   _____

   _____

6. The food smells good.

   _____

7. Jennifer's voice is nice.

   _____

8. He did well.

   _____

Level 8 Unit 8 Description *(Use with pupil book pages 285–287.)*
Skill: Students will rewrite sentences, replacing words with more exact words, similes, or metaphors.

Houghton Mifflin English 8
Copyright © Houghton Mifflin Company. All rights reserved.

Name _____

RETEACHING WORKBOOK 59

COMPOSITION SKILL: DESCRIPTION

Organizing Your Description

There are four main ways to organize a description:
1. Use **spatial order**. Organize the details from nearest to farthest, from farthest to nearest; from left to right, from right to left; from top to bottom, or from bottom to top.
2. Start with the detail that strikes you first.
3. Go from the most important detail to the least important detail.
4. Go from the least important detail to the most important detail.

A. List five vivid details to describe what you are wearing. Arrange the details in spatial order from head to toe.

_____

_____

_____

_____

_____

B. List five vivid details to describe someone important to you. Start with the least important detail and end with the most important one.

_____

_____

_____

_____

_____

C. List five details about what you see and hear outside your house or apartment building in the morning. Start with the detail that strikes you first.

_____

_____

_____

_____

_____

Houghton Mifflin English 8
Copyright © Houghton Mifflin Company. All rights reserved.

Level 8 Unit 8 Description *(Use with pupil book pages 288–289.)*
Skill: Students will list five descriptive details about a person, a place, and a thing, arranging the details in specified orders.

Name _____

RETEACHING WORKBOOK 60

THE WRITING PROCESS: DESCRIPTION

Step 3: Revise

Have I	yes
added sense words to the description?	☐
added exact words and similes or metaphors to the description?	☐
added details that support the point of view and crossed out any that do not?	☐
changed the order of any sentences that do not fit the organization of the description?	☐

Revise the following story. Use the check list above to help you. Check off each box when you have finished your revision.
● Use a thesaurus to help find exact words.
● Use the space above each line, on the sides, and below the paragraph for your changes.

I could tell from Russell's room that he liked sports. By the

door where I walked in was some equipment. Next to that was

a uniform. On the far wall was a sports poster. Between me and

the far wall was a shelf full of things the person had won. They

had been polished and were incredibly shiny. There were books

about monster movies on the shelf too. The lamp under the

poster was shaped like a piece of sports equipment.

Level 8 Unit 8 Description   (Use with pupil book pages 293–294.)
Skill: Students will revise a description, adding sense words, exact words, and figurative language, checking that details support the point of view, and reordering sentences to fit the paragraph's organization.

Houghton Mifflin English 8
Copyright © Houghton Mifflin Company. All rights reserved.

Name _____

RETEACHING WORKBOOK **61**

THE WRITING PROCESS: DESCRIPTION

Step 4: Proofread

When you proofread, look for mistakes in spelling, capitalization, punctuation, and grammar. Use proofreading marks to make corrections.

Jans radio is ~~more~~ smaller than mine but it is real powerful.

Proofreading Marks				
¶ Indent.	⌃ Add a comma.	⊙ Add a period.	≡ Capitalize.	Add quotation marks.
⋀ Add something.	∼ Reverse the order.	℘ Take out.	/ Make a small letter.	

A. Proofread the following paragraph. There are three spelling errors, two incorrect adjectives, one capitalization error, and one punctuation error. Correct the errors. Use a dictionary to check your spelling.

The better vacation I have ever had was spent at my grandparents' house on the banks of the Ohio river. When I sat on the porch, I could hear the breeze whispering through the leafs of the trees. I lisened to the river. Sometimes it made soft lapping noises and other times it made furyous rushing sounds. Grandpa told sailing stories. Of all the sounds, his voice was the most soothingest.

B. Proofread the following paragraph. There are two spelling errors, one incorrect adjective, one incorrect adverb, one capitalization error, and one punctuation error. Correct the errors.

When you open the door to the Main Street Diner, the smell always rushes out and flows around you. It is a gloryous mixture of fresh bread, onions, stew, and calfs' liver. the smell of garlic is real overpowering and it makes all the food more temptinger than ever.

Houghton Mifflin English 8
Copyright © Houghton Mifflin Company. All rights reserved.

Level 8 Unit 8 Description *(Use with pupil book pages 295–296.)*
Skill: Students will proofread paragraphs, correcting mistakes in spelling, capitalization, punctuation, and grammar.

Name _____   **RETEACHING WORKBOOK**   **63**

MECHANICS

1 | Sentences and Interjections

> ▶ Every sentence begins with a **capital letter**.
> ▶ Use a **period** after a declarative or an imperative sentence.
> ▶ Use a **question mark** after an interrogative sentence.
> ▶ Use an **exclamation point** after an exclamatory sentence and after an interjection that shows strong feeling.
> ▶ Use a **comma** after an interjection that shows mild feeling.
>
> **Declarative:**   **M**y, Stevenson's *Treasure Island* is a great book**.**
> **Interrogative:** **H**ave you read this book**?**
> **Imperative:**   **P**lease take my copy**.**
> **Exclamatory:**   **W**ow**! W**hat an adventure Jim Hawkins had**!**

Rewrite each sentence, using correct capitalization and end punctuation.

Example: do you like stories about pirates

   Do you like stories about pirates? _____

1. oh, yes I enjoyed reading *Treasure Island*

   _____

2. wow what an exciting story it was

   _____

3. tell me what happened in the end

   _____

4. no you should read the story yourself

   _____

5. was there really treasure on Treasure Island

   _____

6. did Jim Hawkins deal with dangerous pirates

   _____

7. tell me your opinion of the book

   _____

Level 8   Unit 9   Capitalization and Punctuation   *(Use with pupil book page 304.)*
Skill: Students will capitalize and will punctuate the four types of sentences.

Name _____ RETEACHING WORKBOOK **64**

MECHANICS

2 | **Proper Nouns and Proper Adjectives**

> ▶ A proper noun begins with a capital letter.
> ▶ You can form proper adjectives from proper nouns.
> ▶ Capitalize proper adjectives.
>
> **People:** Senator J. Lopez, Uncle Ed   **Languages:** German, Spanish
> **Places:** Gulf of Tonkin, the West   **School Subjects:** Biology 101
> **Days and Months:** Monday, June   **Events:** Civil War
> **Organizations:** National Football League **Periods of Time:** Dark Ages
> **Institutions:** University of Illinois   **Documents:** Treaty of Paris
> **Proper Adjectives:** French bread, Turkish towel, June wedding

Write each group of words correctly, capitalizing the proper nouns and proper adjectives.

Example: west of ames, iowa   _____ west of Ames, Iowa _____

1. route 3 _____

2. fourth of july _____

3. middle ages _____

4. american canoe association _____

5. alma college in michigan _____

6. a saturday in the spring _____

7. mrs. canard's french accent _____

8. boston tea party in 1773 _____

9. sydney opera house in australia _____

10. death valley in the west _____

11. mom's uncle, uncle jake _____

12. south of baffin bay _____

13. idaho potatoes at ted's grocery _____

14. science with dr. amy jurigian _____

15. geology 1 at brown university _____

16. a bengal tiger from india _____

Level 8   Unit 9   Capitalization and Punctuation   *(Use with pupil book pages 305–307.)*
Skill: Students will capitalize proper nouns and proper adjectives.

Name _____   **RETEACHING WORKBOOK** 65

MECHANICS

3 | Uses for Commas

> ► Use a comma to separate items in a series.
> ► Use a comma between two or more adjectives that come before a noun. Do not use a comma if they express a single idea.
> ► Use a comma to separate simple sentences within a compound sentence.
>
> Terry likes beautiful, solemn music.
> She plays music with Ned, Jo, and Ping.
> They play in the morning, at night, and on weekends.
> Ping plays the piano, Ned sings, and Jo strums the guitar.

Rewrite each sentence, adding commas where they are needed.

Example: Terry has recordings of Mozart Brahms and Bach.

Terry has recordings of Mozart, Brahms, and Bach.

1. Terry loves playing the piano and she loves listening to records.

   _____

2. She owns old new and rare recordings.

   _____

3. Terry buys records in stores at fairs and at yard sales.

   _____

4. One record store sells fragile unusual records.

   _____

5. The owners keep the old rare recordings in a glass case.

   _____

6. Terry loves the recordings of Caruso McCormick and Fitzgerald.

   _____

7. The record store sells records rents videos and shows films.

   _____

8. Terry buys records Ned rents videos and Jo attends films there.

   _____

Level 8   Unit 9   Capitalization and Punctuation   *(Use with pupil book pages 308–309.)*
Skill: Students will use commas in a series and in compound sentences.

Houghton Mifflin English 8
Copyright © Houghton Mifflin Company. All rights reserved.

Name _____ **RETEACHING WORKBOOK** **66**

MECHANICS

4 | **More Uses for Commas**

▶ Use commas after words, phrases, and clauses that come at the beginning of sentences.
▶ Use commas to separate interrupters, nouns of direct address, and unnecessary appositives in a sentence.

> **Introductory Word:** Yes, a musician must have good timing.
> **Introductory Phrase:** Before a piano recital, students practice.
> **Introductory Clause:** While Linda plays, she often composes.
> **Interrupter:** A composer, of course, must have talent.
> **Noun of Direct Address:** Can you read music, Linda?
> **Appositives:** Linda Granges, a composer, arranged this music.
> She also wrote the song "Willow Tree."

Rewrite each sentence, adding commas where they are needed.

Example: Sue Ling a piano student writes songs as well.

Sue Ling, a piano student, writes songs as well.

1. Say did you know that Sue has written many wonderful songs?

   _____

2. Before Sue wrote any songs she listened to a lot of music.

   _____

3. Linda her song "Soaring" has been recently published.

   _____

4. An ability to read music of course helps musicians.

   _____

5. During each piano lesson Sue usually takes notes.

   _____

6. Most professional composers study music for a long time you see.

   _____

7. Sue a serious musician has studied music since she was seven.

   _____

Level 8 Unit 9 Capitalization and Punctuation *(Use with pupil book pages 310–311.)*
Skill: Students will use commas to set off interrupters and introductory words, phrases, and clauses.

Name _____ RETEACHING WORKBOOK 67

MECHANICS

5 | Dates, Addresses, and Letters

> ▸ Use a comma to separate the month and the day from the year.
> ▸ Use a comma between the city and the state. Use a comma after the state if the address is within the sentence. Use a comma to separate each item except the ZIP Code.
> ▸ Use a comma after the greeting in friendly letters and after the closing in both friendly and business letters.
>
> **Dates and Addresses**　　**Greetings and Closings**
> July 16, 1990　　　　　　　Dear Dinah,
> 1002 Madison Avenue　　　Your sister,
> New York, NY 10022　　　Sincerely yours,

Rewrite the letter, adding commas where they are needed.

　　　　　　　　　　　　　　　　　　　　　　122 First Street
　　　　　　　　　　　　　　　　　　　　　　Teaneck New Jersey 07666
　　　　　　　　　　　　　　　　　　　　　　May 29 1990

Dear Carmela,

　　I found the facts that you requested on May 16 1990 in Chicago Illinois. Woodrow Wilson was born in Staunton Virginia on December 28 1856. In June 1902 Wilson became president of Princeton University. Later he lived at the White House. That address is 1600 Pennsylvania Avenue Washington D.C. 20013.

　　　　　　　　　　　　　　　　　　　　　　Sincerely yours
　　　　　　　　　　　　　　　　　　　　　　Stanley

Level 8　Unit 9　Capitalization and Punctuation　　(Use with pupil book pages 312–313.)
Skill:　Students will use commas in dates and addresses in a letter.

Name _____   RETEACHING WORKBOOK   **68**

MECHANICS

6 | **Quotation Marks**

> ► Use quotation marks to set off direct quotations from the rest of the sentence.
> ► Use quotation marks around the titles of short stories, poems, book chapters, magazine articles, and songs.
> ► Capitalize all important words in a title.
>
> **Direct Quotations:**   "Deer are lovely animals," said Chen.
>   Did Nora say, "I have watched wild deer"?
> **Indirect Quotation:** Nora said that she has photographed deer.
> **Title of a Short Work:** Chen read the article "Deer in the North."

Rewrite each sentence, using correct capitalization and punctuation. The direct quotations are underlined to help you.

Example: Susan said I like deer.   _Susan said, "I like deer."_

1. Chen said male deer grow new antlers each spring.

   _____

2. The article deer move north gives interesting facts about deer.

   _____

3. Bucks stated Chen have powerful legs.

   _____

4. Deer can run more than thirty miles an hour explained Tony.

   _____

5. Deer can detect motion said Chen. Their sense of smell is sharp.

   _____

6. Did Susan say tell me what a deer looks like?

   _____

7. Chen said that the poem fawn and the story spots are about deer.

   _____

8. Do deer make sounds asked Susan.

   _____

Level 8 Unit 9 Capitalization and Punctuation   *(Use with pupil book pages 314–316.)*
Skill: Students will capitalize and will punctuate direct quotations and titles of short works.

Name _____ RETEACHING WORKBOOK 69

MECHANICS

7 | Titles of Long Works

> ▶ Underline the titles of major works like books, magazines, newspapers, plays, movies, television series, works of art, and long musical compositions.
> ▶ Capitalize all important words in a title.
>
> My sister's favorite play is <u>**H**amlet</u>.
> Monet's <u>**T**he **W**ater **L**ily **P**ond</u> is in the Denver Art Museum.
> Our class took a field trip to see the movie <u>**T**he **S**ound of **M**usic</u>.

Write these titles of long works correctly.

Example: a separate peace _____ A Separate Peace _____

1. the prince and the pauper

2. symphony no. 3

3. creative teens

4. a raisin in the sun

5. chariots of fire

6. madam butterfly

7. usa today

8. portrait of paul revere

9. the new york times

10. the once and future king

11. the bill cosby show

12. kitchen still life

13. camelot

14. field and stream

15. fantasia

16. the merchant of venice

17. the brady bunch

18. vermont life

Level 8 Unit 9   Capitalization and Punctuation   (Use with pupil book pages 317–318.)
Skill: Students will capitalize and will punctuate titles of long works.

Name _____ **RETEACHING WORKBOOK** **70**

MECHANICS

8 | Colons and Semicolons

> ▶ Use a **colon** after a greeting in a business letter, between the hour and the minutes in time, and before a list.
> ▶ Use a **semicolon** to connect independent clauses that are closely related in thought or that have **commas** within them.

Colons: Dear Mr. James**:**
The practice begins at 6**:**00 P.M.
Bring the following**:** music, a stand, and your instrument.

Semicolons: I like this piece**;** Ramon doesn't.
Di played the music grandly**;** however, she missed some notes.
Ramon likes jazz, blues, and reggae music**;** and Fran likes
classical, rock, and folk music.

Rewrite the part of the letter shown below, adding colons and semicolons where they are needed. The underlined words are clues to help you.

Dear Mrs. Phelps

 I will be at the audition at 5 00 P.M. I look forward to performing for you
I really want to play in your band. I will play these compositions "Billy's
Bounce," "Donna Lee," and "Blusette." I usually play jazz, blues, and country
however, I play classical music too.
 I understand that your band has four trumpet players, five saxophonists, and four
trombone players but I hope you have room for another trumpet player.

Sincerely,
Ashley Palermo

_____

_____

_____

_____

_____

_____

_____

                              _____

                              _____

Level 8 Unit 9 Capitalization and Punctuation *(Use with pupil book pages 319–320.)*
Skill: Students will use colons and semicolons correctly.

Name _____ RETEACHING WORKBOOK 71

MECHANICS
 Abbreviations and Numbers

> ► Most abbreviations begin with a capital letter and end with a period.
> ► Spell out numbers under one hundred and numbers at the beginning of a sentence. Use numerals for numbers over one hundred and for sections of writing.
>
> **Abbreviations:** Thursday **Thurs.** gallon **gal.**
> Street **St.** Senator **Sen.**
> Corporation **Corp.** Post Office **P.O.**
> Florida **FL** American League **AL**
>
> **Numbers:** **Forty-nine** people had voted by **one** o'clock.
> By **1:55** P.M., **149** people had voted on Question **2**.

A. Write each phrase, using the correct abbreviation for the underlined word or words. Use your dictionary to help you.

Example: Saturday ___Sat.___

1. Nick Rose, Senior _____
2. 9 miles per hour _____
3. Forest Service _____
4. eight o'clock P.M. _____
5. Abt Incorporated _____
6. River High School _____
7. Hays, Kansas _____
8. April 1 _____
9. Wednesday _____
10. 2 Ivy Avenue _____
11. Apartment 7 _____
12. 11 inches _____

B. Rewrite each sentence, correcting the underlined words and numerals.

13. At one-fifty the plane from Dallas arrived with 200 passengers.

_____

14. 1 passenger waved from Gate Six to her waiting family.

_____

15. At 2 o'clock 51 people boarded the airplane.

_____

16. The plane left at two-ten P.M. with two hundred fifty-one passengers.

_____

Level 8 Unit 9 Capitalization and Punctuation (Use with pupil book pages 321–323.)
Skill: Students will write abbreviations and numbers correctly.

Name _____

RETEACHING WORKBOOK **72**

MECHANICS

10 | **Apostrophes**

▶ Add an **apostrophe** and *s* to singular nouns and to plural nouns not end-ing in *s* to show possession. Add an apostrophe to plural nouns ending in *s* to show possession.
▶ Add an apostrophe and *s* to form the plural of letters, numerals, symbols, and words that refer to themselves. Use an apostrophe in contractions.

Possessive Nouns: senator**'s**, Smith**'s**, children**'s**, classmates**'**
Contractions: didn't, wouldn't, they're, we'll
Plurals of Letters, Numerals, and Symbols: *A*'s and *B*'s, *6*'s, *t*'s, *%*'s
Plurals of Names of Words: *and*'s, *good*'s, *remember*'s

Rewrite the sentences, adding apostrophes where they are needed. The under-lined words and symbols are clues to help you.

Example: Bridgets almanac is blue. _____**Bridget's almanac is blue.**_____

1. Janiss almanac has a section on the Olympics.

_____

2. One gymnast in the last Olympics received five *10*s.

_____

3. There are six **s on this list of gold medal winners.

_____

4. Ingemar Stenmarks medal was for the mens slalom.

_____

5. On the list are five gymnasts with two *ss* in their names.

_____

6. My two sisters teacher wants world population figures.

_____

7. The *North*s and the *South*s are incorrectly placed on this map.

_____

8. Theyll confuse many readers. _____

Level 8 Unit 9 Capitalization and Punctuation *(Use with pupil book pages 324–325.)*
Skill: Students will use apostrophes correctly in possessive nouns, contractions, and plurals.

Name _____ **RETEACHING WORKBOOK** **73**

MECHANICS

11 | Hyphens, Dashes, and Parentheses

> ▶ Use a **hyphen** to divide a word at the end of a line, to join the parts of compound numbers, and to join two or more words that work together as one adjective before a noun.
> ▶ Use **dashes** to show a sudden change of thought.
> ▶ Use **parentheses** to enclose unnecessary information.
>
> **Hyphens:** forty-two, two-thirds full, well-deserved praise
> **Dash:** Tim lit the wood stove—Ben Franklin's invention.
> **Parentheses:** Ben Franklin (1706–1790) experimented with electricity.
> Franklin (the inventor) became ambassador to France.

A. Rewrite the sentences, adding hyphens and dashes where they are needed. The underlined words are clues to help you.

Example: He lived <u>eighty four</u> years.   **He lived eighty-four years.**

1. Benjamin Franklin he was a founding father of his country invented many <u>well known</u> items.

_____

_____

2. He was <u>one third</u> statesman, <u>one third</u> writer, and <u>one third</u> inventor.

_____

3. At age <u>eighty one</u> <u>he lived a long life</u> Franklin still actively served his country.

_____

B. Rewrite the sentences, adding parentheses where they are needed. Use the underlined words to help you.

4. Ts'ai Lun <u>a Chinese official</u> invented paper in about A.D. 105.

_____

5. The cotton gin <u>invented by Eli Whitney</u> removes seeds from cotton.

_____

6. Thomas Edison <u>1847–1931</u> improved the electric light bulb.

_____

Level 8 Unit 9 Capitalization and Punctuation   *(Use with pupil book pages 326–327.)*
Skill: Students will use hyphens, dashes, and parentheses correctly.

Name _____ **RETEACHING WORKBOOK** **75**

COMPOSITION SKILL: PERSUASIVE LETTER

Writing Business Letters

A **business letter** is a formal letter written for a purpose, such as to apply for a job, to order something, to request information, or to complain about a product or a service. The letter should be polite and to the point and should include all necessary information. A business letter has six parts: heading, inside address, greeting, body, closing, and signature. The greeting is followed by a colon *(:).* Write a business letter in block or modified block style.

Write a business letter to the president of Business Bank of Bethel at 427 Lake Avenue in Bethel, Maine 04217. Tell the president that you are interested in starting a bike messenger service. Ask for information about starting and managing a small business. Use your own name and address and today's date.

_____

_____

_____

_____

_____

_____

_____

_____

_____

_____

_____

_____

_____

_____

_____

Houghton Mifflin English 8
Copyright © Houghton Mifflin Company. All rights reserved.

UNIT 10 PERSUASIVE LETTER

Level 8 Unit 10 Persuasive Letter *(Use with pupil book pages 357–359.)*
Skill: Students will write a business letter, requesting information.

Name _____   **RETEACHING WORKBOOK**   **76**

COMPOSITION SKILL: PERSUASIVE LETTER

Stating and Supporting an Opinion

> When you write to persuade, state your opinion clearly and support it with reasons and factual examples. Suit your reasons to your audience.

A. Imagine that you are a salesperson at the Viper-1 car dealership. Below are some possible reasons you could use to support the opinion *You should buy a Viper-1 car.* Underline the reason that best answers each question below.

1. Which of the following reasons would best persuade a customer with four children?
    a. The Viper-1 has a four-speed transmission and fuel injection.
    b. The Viper-1 has hand-tooled leather seats and walnut paneling.
    c. The Viper-1 seats six and has a huge trunk.

2. Which of the following reasons is not related to the opinion?
    a. The Viper-1 commercials are some of the best on TV.
    b. The Viper-1 offers a five-year guarantee.
    c. The Viper-1 averages forty miles per gallon of gas.

3. Which of the following is a provable fact?
    a. The Viper-1 was named Car of the Year by *Car Critic* magazine.
    b. The Viper-1 gives the most comfortable ride of any car on the road.
    c. The Viper factory employs only the best engineers and mechanics.

4. Which of the following reasons is stated most strongly and clearly?
    a. The buyers I've talked with seem content with their Viper-1 cars.
    b. We've sold six hundred Viper-1 cars this year without a single complaint.
    c. You'll probably like the Viper-1 a lot once you get used to it.

B. Read the following paragraph. Underline the opinion. Then list three supporting reasons.

I think our club dues should be put in a savings account. Our dues would then earn interest, which would give us more money to spend later. It would also be safer in a bank than in a cracker tin in an unlocked room. If the money is easy for us to get, we would be more likely to spend it and less likely to save it. A savings account makes good business sense to me!

_____

_____

_____

Level 8 Unit 10   Persuasive Letter   *(Use with pupil book pages 361–362.)*
Skill: Students will identify reasons that fit given standards and will identify an opinion and supporting reasons in a persuasive letter.

Name _____

RETEACHING WORKBOOK **77**

COMPOSITION SKILL: PERSUASIVE LETTER

Using Persuasive Strategies

When you have an opinion and reasons that support it, use these persuasive strategies in your argument.

Offer a precedent, or refer to a similar situation as an example.
Appeal to fairness with a solid example.
Overcome objections by answering them before they are raised.
Explore consequences by naming good results your idea might have and overcoming unfavorable results.

Read the following part of a letter written to support the opinion stated in the first paragraph. Look for persuasive strategies. Then use the sentences from the letter to answer the questions below.

Dear Editor:

The legal driving age should be fifteen. Here are my reasons.

The present law concerning the age limit was made when teen-agers had few places to go. Driving is more important now, and I think it is only fair to reconsider the age limit.

I know that fourteen-year-olds lack experience. However, they would quickly gain it. Younger drivers also have better eyesight and reflexes than older drivers.

When cars were first being driven, there were no age limits for drivers. Many teen-agers drove. There were also far fewer accidents in those days.

Driving would allow young people to see more of the world. They also could help their parents by doing chores that demand a car.

Sincerely,

Mort Simmons

1. Which sentence offers a precedent? _____

_____

2. Which sentence appeals to fairness? _____

_____

3. Which sentence overcomes an objection? _____

_____

4. Which sentence explores consequences? _____

_____

Level 8 Unit 10 Persuasive Letter *(Use with pupil book pages 363–364.)*
Skill: Students will identify common persuasive strategies.

Houghton Mifflin English 8
Copyright © Houghton Mifflin Company. All rights reserved.

Name _____ **RETEACHING WORKBOOK** **78**

COMPOSITION SKILL: PERSUASIVE LETTER

Shaping Your Argument

> Begin a persuasive paragraph with a clear topic sentence. Support your opinion with reasons arranged in an **order of importance** that will suit your audience. The order may be from most to least important or from least to most important. Finish with a strong summary statement.

A. Suppose that you have just learned about a new football helmet. You want to convince your coach to let your team try these new helmets. Place a check beside the sentence or sentences that answer each question below.

1. Which topic sentence states the opinion more clearly?

   a. _____ Kango helmets can help our team in more ways than one.

   b. _____ You should look at this new line of helmets.

2. Which three reasons below would be most likely to convince a coach?

   a. _____ Kangoes weigh half as much as ordinary helmets.

   b. _____ Kangoes are made by a European company that once made knight's armor.

   c. _____ Kangoes cost a little more than ordinary helmets.

   d. _____ Kangoes reduce head and neck injuries by eighty per cent.

   e. _____ Kangoes feature a new design with a permanent, scratch-proof finish.

3. Which is the stronger summary statement?

   a. _____ As you can see, the new Kango helmets are quite attractive.

   b. _____ A Kango helmet is a winner in performance and safety.

B. Using your choices above, write a paragraph to persuade your coach to try Kango helmets. Write your supporting reasons in least to most important order.

_____

_____

_____

_____

_____

_____

Level 8   Unit 10   Persuasive Letter   *(Use with pupil book pages 364–365.)*
Skill: Students will choose a strong topic sentence, suitable reasons, and a strong summary statement, and will write a persuasive paragraph based on those choices.

Name _____

RETEACHING WORKBOOK 79

THE WRITING PROCESS: PERSUASIVE LETTER

Step 3: Revise

Have I	yes
added a topic sentence that clearly states the opinion?	☐
added supporting reasons and specific examples, including a reason that overcomes an objection or that offers a precedent?	☐
crossed out reasons that are weak or not relevant and checked that supporting reasons are in a convincing order?	☐
added a concluding statement that emphasizes or restates the opinion?	☐

Revise the following persuasive letter. Use the check list above to help you. Check off each box when you have finished your revision.
• Use the space above each line, on the sides, and below the paragraph for your changes.

Dear Mr. Pick:

You don't know me, but I'm writing to you anyway. I've

heard a lot about you. My friend Carla Rizzo, a student of

yours, says that you're the best guitar teacher. I want to take

lessons. I have my own guitar and have been playing for a while

on my own. I hope to be a professional musician someday. If

not, maybe I will work as an artist or in the computer field. I

can't afford to pay much, but Carla says that you sometimes

lower your rates for good students. I'll work hard.

Houghton Mifflin English 8
Copyright © Houghton Mifflin Company. All rights reserved.

Level 8 Unit 10 Persuasive Letter *(Use with pupil book pages 369–370.)*
Skill: Students will revise a persuasive letter, adding a topic sentence, supporting reasons, and specific examples, checking that reasons are relevant and in order, and adding a concluding statement.

Name _____

RETEACHING WORKBOOK 80

THE WRITING PROCESS: PERSUASIVE LETTER

Step 4: Proofread

When you proofread, look for mistakes in spelling, capitalization, and punctuation. Use proofreading marks to make corrections.

please put me on your Mailing list i want to receive pamphlets on water safety

Proofreading Marks				
¶ Indent.	∧ Add a comma.	⊙ Add a period.	≡ Capitalize.	Add quotation marks.
∧ Add something.	∽ Reverse the order.	ℐ Take out.	/ Make a small letter.	

Proofread this business letter. There are two spelling errors, four capitalization errors, four punctuation errors, one incorrectly written number, and two errors in abbreviation. Correct the errors. Use a dictionary to check your spelling.

70 Tumbleweed road

Cave Creek AZ 85331

August 2, 1990

Oceans Unlimited, Inc

101 Coral drive

Alturas FL 33820

Dear Sir or madam,

This is in response to your ad in the july issue of Splash magazine.

Please send me the s.c.u.b.a. outfit advertised. I am enclosing the $ fifty

shipping cost required.   I understand that the balance of $315.00 is to be paid

COD. I except this arrangement

Level 8 Unit 10 **Persuasive Letter** *(Use with pupil book pages 371–372.)*
Skill: Students will proofread a business letter, correcting mistakes in spelling, capitalization, and punctuation.

Name _____   **RETEACHING WORKBOOK** **81**

LANGUAGE AND USAGE

1 | Personal and Possessive Pronouns

> ▶ A **pronoun** is used to replace a noun.
> ▶ **Personal pronouns** have different forms to show person, number, and gender.
> ▶ A **possessive pronoun** can replace a possessive noun.
>
> | | first | second | third |
> |---|---|---|---|
> | **Person:** | I like sewing. | **You** like singing. | **They** like painting. |
>
> | | singular | plural |
> |---|---|---|
> | **Number:** | Marcia teaches **him**. | Marcia teaches **them**. |
>
> | | masculine | feminine | neuter |
> |---|---|---|---|
> | **Gender:** | **He** is a sculptor. | **She** is a sculptor. | **It** is a sculpture. |
>
> **Possessive:** The class admires **her** work. That design is **hers**.

A. Label each underlined pronoun *first person, second person,* or *third person.* Then label it *singular* or *plural.*

Example: Ms. Gray teaches <u>us</u> silk-screening. _____first person, plural_____

1. <u>We</u> make prints on paper and cloth. _____

2. Do <u>you</u> two like the designs? _____

3. Please help <u>me</u> prepare two screens. _____

4. <u>They</u> are usually made of silk. _____

5. <u>It</u> is a fascinating printing technique. _____

6. Sid, would <u>you</u> like to join the class? _____

7. Marcia can show <u>him</u> how to begin. _____

8. <u>She</u> is a good teacher and artist. _____

B. Write the correct word in parentheses to complete each sentence.

Example: Do you like _____your_____ Saturday class? (your, you're)

9. The class is having _____ first art show. (it's, its)

10. The students created _____ own designs. (their, they're)

11. Amanda is exhibiting _____ prints. (her, hers)

12. Cassie is exhibiting _____ too. (her, hers)

13. The prints in the corner are _____ . (there's, theirs)

14. _____ are the ones by the window. (My, Mine)

Level 8 Unit 11 Pronouns *(Use with pupil book pages 380–382.)*
Skill: Students will identify the person and number of personal pronouns and will use possessive pronouns correctly.

Houghton Mifflin English 8
Copyright © Houghton Mifflin Company. All rights reserved.

UNIT 11 PRONOUNS

Name _____ **RETEACHING WORKBOOK** **82**

LANGUAGE AND USAGE

2 | Pronoun Antecedents

> ▶ An **antecedent** is a noun or a pronoun to which a pronoun refers.
> ▶ A pronoun must agree with its antecedent in person, number, and gender.
>
> People applauded. **They** were ready to enjoy the play.
> They grew quiet, and an announcer welcomed **them**.
> Although **it** was simple, the set was beautiful.
> Both the star and the minor characters knew **their** parts.
> Would the stage manager or the prompters forget **their** jobs?

A. Complete each sentence, using the pronoun that agrees with the underlined antecedent or antecedents.

Example: The <u>actors</u> gave _____**their**_____ best performance. **(her, their)**

1. <u>Sarah Bernhardt</u> was a famous French actress. Thousands of fans admired

   _____ . **(them, her)**

2. Sarah had <u>talent</u> and <u>beauty</u>, and _____ drew praise from the critics. **(it, they)**

3. Did <u>Sarah</u> or other <u>performers</u> of the time use _____ talents in movies as well? **(her, their)**

B. Rewrite the sentences so that the antecedents of the underlined pronouns are clear.

Example: <u>They</u> followed Sarah's career for sixty years.

   Fans followed Sarah's career for sixty years. _____

4. When she was on stage, Sarah made <u>it</u> seem so easy.

   _____

5. <u>They</u> say that Sarah could have played any role well.

   _____

6. My grandmother saw Sarah Bernhardt perform when <u>she</u> was a girl.

   _____

Level 8 Unit 11 Pronouns *(Use with pupil book pages 383–385.)*
Skill: Students will choose pronouns to agree with their antecedents and will correct sentences with unclear antecedents.

Name _____

RETEACHING WORKBOOK **83**

LANGUAGE AND USAGE

3 | Pronoun Case

> ▶ Subject pronouns are in the **nominative case**.
> ▶ Use the nominative case for pronouns used as subjects and predicate pronouns.
> ▶ Object pronouns are in the **objective case**.
> ▶ Use the objective case for pronouns used as direct objects and indirect objects.
>
> subject
> **Nominative:** My friends and **I** admire Anna Pavlova's career.
>
> predicate pronoun
> Our favorite dancer is **she**.
>
> direct object
> **Objective:** Pavlova's career fascinates **us**.
>
> indirect object   indirect object
> Please lend **her** and **me** the book about Pavlova.

Write the correct pronoun forms in parentheses to complete these sentences.

Example: Carmen and (I, me) saw a film about Anna Pavlova.   _____I_____

1. The film inspired her and (I, me). _____

2. (She, Her) and I both study ballet. _____

3. It is (she, her) who has studied the longest. _____

4. (We, Us) and the other students in our class work hard. _____

5. Mr. Armado teaches (they, them) and (we, us) difficult steps. _____

6. It was (he, him) who suggested the film about Pavlova. _____

7. Great challenges faced (she, her). _____

8. Pavlova never gave (they, them) a chance to discourage her. _____

9. (She, Her) and her partners practiced constantly. _____

10. Pavlova and (they, them) could not depend upon talent alone. _____

11. Mr. Armado is strict, but now we appreciate (he, him) more. _____

12. The people in need of the most practice are (we, us). _____

Level 8   Unit 11   **Pronouns**   *(Use with pupil book pages 386–388.)*
Skill: Students will choose pronouns in the nominative and the objective cases to complete sentences.

Houghton Mifflin English 8
Copyright © Houghton Mifflin Company. All rights reserved.

Name _____

RETEACHING WORKBOOK 84

LANGUAGE AND USAGE

4 | Interrogative Pronouns

> ▶ **Interrogative pronouns** like *who, which, what, whom,* and *whose* ask questions.
> ▶ Use *who* as a subject, *whom* as an object, and *whose* as a possessive.
> ▶ Do not confuse the pronoun *whose* with the contraction *who's.*
>
> **Who** are the reporters? **Whom** are they following?
> **Whose** is that uniform? **Who's** the pilot?

Complete each sentence, using the correct word in parentheses.

Example: _____Who_____ is Sally Ride? **(Who, Whom)**

1. _____ are the other astronauts? **(Who, Whom)**

2. _____ did the President meet? **(Who, Whom)**

3. _____ is the spacecraft to be launched? **(Which, Whom)**

4. _____ is that silver helmet? **(Who's, Whose)**

5. _____ checking the spacecraft? **(Who's, Whose)**

6. _____ was the problem? **(What, Whom)**

7. _____ is the youngest astronaut? **(Who, Whom)**

8. _____ are the most demanding roles on board? **(Who's, Whose)**

9. _____ did the reporters interview? **(Who, Whom)**

10. _____ had the most experience in space? **(Who's, Whose)**

11. _____ will this mission accomplish? **(What, Who)**

12. _____ was chosen to leave the space capsule? **(Who, Whom)**

13. _____ can the astronauts contact on Earth? **(Who, Whom)**

14. _____ was the longest space flight? **(Which, Whom)**

15. _____ is that voice on the loudspeaker? **(Who's, Whose)**

16. _____ decides the purpose of the flight? **(Who, Whom)**

17. _____ taking photographs of the liftoff? **(Who's, Whose)**

18. _____ should we ask for more information? **(Who, Whom)**

Level 8 Unit 11 Pronouns *(Use with pupil book pages 389–390.)*
Skill: Students will use interrogative pronouns and *who's* correctly.

Houghton Mifflin English 8
Copyright © Houghton Mifflin Company. All rights reserved.

Name _____ **RETEACHING WORKBOOK** 85

LANGUAGE AND USAGE

5 | Demonstrative Pronouns

> ▶ A **demonstrative pronoun** points out persons, places, things, or ideas.
> ▶ *This* and *that* refer to singular nouns or pronouns.
> ▶ *These* and *those* refer to plural nouns or pronouns.
> ▶ *This* and *these* point out things that are close.
> ▶ *That* and *those* point out things that are farther away.
>
> **This** is a double-decker bus.   **These** are double-decker buses.
> **That** is a bus across the street.   **Those** are the buses over there.

Rewrite the sentences, using the correct words in parentheses.

Example: (This, These) is the city of London.

This is the city of London.

1. Are (this, these) the maps of the city?

   _____

2. (This, That) looks like Big Ben right here.

   _____

3. (That, Those) are the hedges surrounding Kensington Park.

   _____

4. Isn't (this, that) Buckingham Palace across the park?

   _____

5. (These here, These) are tourists hoping to see the queen.

   _____

6. (This, These) is the entrance to the underground.

   _____

7. (That there, That) is our train to the West End.

   _____

8. (Those there, Those) are the famous West End statues.

   _____

Level 8 Unit 11 Pronouns   *(Use with pupil book pages 391–392.)*
Skill: Students will use demonstrative pronouns correctly.

Name _____   **RETEACHING WORKBOOK**   **86**

LANGUAGE AND USAGE

6 | Indefinite Pronouns

> ▶ An **indefinite pronoun** does not refer to a specific person or thing.
> ▶ Verbs must agree in number with indefinite pronouns used as subjects.
>   Pronouns must agree with indefinite pronouns used as antecedents.
>
> **Singular:** **Everyone** is reading the same science book.
>   **Most** of the book has interesting information in it.
> **Plural:** **Several** of the students use the book on field trips.
>   **Most** of my classmates take the book with them on the trips.

Rewrite each sentence, using the word in parentheses that agrees with the underlined indefinite pronoun.

Example: Many of the exhibits (sounds, sound) interesting.

Many of the exhibits sound interesting.

1. Everybody (thinks, think) that the science trips are very good.

   _____

2. Many of us (looks, look) forward to these trips.

   _____

3. Some of the information is new, and students take notes on (it, them).

   _____

4. Someone (is, are) now organizing a trip to the Botanical Gardens.

   _____

5. Most of the rocks there have fossil plants and animals in (it, them).

   _____

6. Both of the eighth grade science classes (plans, plan) to go.

   _____

7. Nobody in the eighth grade (has, have) ever seen a botanical garden.

   _____

8. Each of our trips has had (its, their) own special attraction.

   _____

Level 8 Unit 11 **Pronouns**   *(Use with pupil book pages 393–396.)*
Skill: Students will choose verbs and pronouns to agree with indefinite pronouns.

Name _____ RETEACHING WORKBOOK 87

LANGUAGE AND USAGE

 7 | **Reflexive and Intensive Pronouns**

> ▶ A **reflexive pronoun** ends in *-self* or *-selves* and refers to the subject of the sentence. It generally cannot be left out of the sentence.
> ▶ An **intensive pronoun** ends in *-self* or *-selves* and emphasizes another word in the sentence. Avoid using pronouns with *-self* or *-selves* as personal pronouns.
>
> **Reflexive:** Maria made **herself** a printing block.
> **Intensive:** The block **itself** was very interesting.

Rewrite each sentence, using the correct pronoun in parentheses.

Example: I found (me, myself) looking at some greeting cards.
I found myself looking at some greeting cards.

1. Mario designed these greeting cards (hisself, himself).
   _____

2. He gave (me, myself) a copy of each one.
   _____

3. Several of us taught (us, ourselves) how to make printing blocks.
   _____

4. You might want to try it (yourself, yourselves), Robby.
   _____

5. When the project began, I asked (me, myself) if I would complete it.
   _____

6. Mario and (I, myself) have a new idea for a design.
   _____

7. I (me, myself) prefer to do the actual carving of the block.
   _____

8. The carved blocks (theirselves, themselves) are very attractive.
   _____

Level 8 Unit 11 Pronouns   (Use with pupil book pages 397–399.)
Skill: Students will use reflexive pronouns, intensive pronouns, and personal pronouns correctly.

Name _____

RETEACHING WORKBOOK **88**

LANGUAGE AND USAGE

8 | Choosing the Right Pronoun

▶ If you use *we* or *us* with a noun, use the pronoun case that you would use if the noun were not there.

▶ To decide which pronoun form to use in an incomplete comparison, add words to complete the comparison.

We students are working hard. *(We are working hard.)*
Nobody disturbs **us** students in the library. *(Nobody disturbs us.)*

I like the work more than **he**. *(I like the work more than he does.)*
I like the work more than **him**. *(I like the work more than I like him.)*

Rewrite each sentence, using the correct pronoun in parentheses.

Example: Ernie is a harder worker than (he, him).

<u>**Ernie is a harder worker than he.**</u>

1. Exam time always affects (we, us) students.

    _____

2. (We, Us) students really must get to work.

    _____

3. Nobody knows that more than (I, me).

    _____

4. Kira always does better on her exams than (I, me).

    _____

5. (We, Us) eighth graders have to study harder than the seventh graders.

    _____

6. More time is given them than (we, us).

    _____

7. Ms. LaPlace is giving (we, us) French students special help.

    _____

8. Last year the German students had much higher scores than (we, us).

    _____

Level 8 Unit 11 Pronouns   *(Use with pupil book pages 400–401.)*
Skill: Students will use pronouns with nouns and in incomplete comparisons.

Name _____ **RETEACHING WORKBOOK** **89**

COMPOSITION SKILL: RESEARCH REPORT

Finding and Narrowing a Topic

Before you write a report, find a topic that really interests you and that will interest your readers. Be sure that you can find information on the topic easily and that it is narrow enough for a short report. Narrow your topic by choosing just one aspect of it or by asking questions about it until you narrow the topic to what interests you most.

Put a check next to the topic in each group that is narrow enough for a short report. Then, for each group, write a topic of your own that is narrow enough for a short report.

1. _____ American movies

   _____ Movies

   _____ Some famous American science-fiction movies of the 1950s

   Narrowed Topic: _____

2. _____ Different types of storms

   _____ How a hurricane forms

   _____ Types of weather

   Narrowed Topic: _____

3. _____ Great mountains of the world

   _____ Mount Everest

   _____ The first successful climb of Mount Everest

   Narrowed Topic: _____

4. _____ A day in the life of a Japanese high-school student

   _____ What high schools are like in different countries of the world

   _____ Schools throughout history

   Narrowed Topic: _____

5. _____ Classic American cars

   _____ The Model T—a classic American car

   _____ Classic cars around the world

   Narrowed Topic: _____

Level 8 Unit 12 Research Report *(Use with pupil book pages 432–433.)*
Skill: Students will identify topics narrow enough for short reports and will write narrowed topics of their own.

Name _____

RETEACHING WORKBOOK 90

COMPOSITION SKILL: RESEARCH REPORT

Planning and Researching a Report

Plan your report by first asking yourself what you want to know about your topic and then looking for the answers in appropriate reference sources.

An **encyclopedia** contains articles on many subjects. An **atlas** contains maps and tables that show population and geographical information. An **almanac** contains up-to-date information on many subjects. A **dictionary** contains not only words but also biographical and geographical information. A **biographical reference book** contains information about people. The *Readers' Guide to Periodical Literature* lists articles published in periodicals. A **nonfiction book** is a factual book on a subject. A **newspaper** contains news stories on current topics.

Write *encyclopedia, atlas, almanac, dictionary, biographical reference, Readers' Guide, nonfiction book,* or *newspaper* to tell where you would look for the answer to each of the following questions.

1. Is Rome, Italy, near the mountains or near the sea? _____

2. When was the first piano made? _____

3. How many people live in France? _____

4. When did Hank Aaron set his home-run record? _____

5. What recent articles discuss Halley's comet? _____

6. What does a lute look like? _____

7. Where did writer Nikki Giovanni grow up? _____

8. How are tunnels built? _____

9. What are the latest published data on cancer research? _____

10. What are the habits of the gnu? _____

11. What major highway connects Hartford and Boston? _____

12. What profession paid the highest average salary last year? _____

13. How many feet are there in a kilometer? _____

14. Who was Mary Pickford? _____

15. What was Lucille Ball's childhood like? _____

16. Who was elected to the United States Senate yesterday? _____

Level 8 Unit 12 Research Report *(Use with pupil book pages 434–436.)*
Skill: Students will identify the best reference source to find a particular type of information.

Houghton Mifflin English 8
Copyright © Houghton Mifflin Company. All rights reserved.

Name _____

COMPOSITION SKILL: RESEARCH REPORT

RETEACHING WORKBOOK 91

Taking Notes

> Before you start taking notes, make a list of questions you would like to answer. As you read, look for the answers to your questions. Write each question on a separate note card, and then write brief answers in your own words, based on what you have read.

Read the following paragraphs. Take notes below to answer the question *Besides management of timber resources, what does a forester do?*

In addition to the careful harvesting, planting, and breeding of timber resources, foresters have other jobs. One of these jobs concerns water. Forests are known as *watersheds*. The soil of a forest is porous and allows water from rain and snow to enter the ground and gradually pass into springs, streams, and rivers. Foresters keep the soil porous by planting trees and shrubs in bare areas. They also regulate the grazing of livestock. Overgrazing can damage watersheds.

Just as it is important to keep a balance of trees in the forest, a balance of wildlife is necessary. Squirrels and birds can live in tall trees, but ground animals need bushes and shrubs to survive. Foresters clear areas of tall trees to permit the growth of low plants. They intentionally leave hollow logs as potential homes for animals.

Most foresters are best known for being fire spotters and firefighters. However, there are times when foresters start fires. This type of fire is called *prescribed burning*. Foresters start these small fires in order to eliminate some of the brush that may fuel a real fire.

_____
_____
_____
_____
_____
_____

Level 8 Unit 12 Research Report (Use with pupil book pages 437–438.)
Skill: Students will read a selection and will take notes to answer a question about it.

Name _____ **RETEACHING WORKBOOK** 92

COMPOSITION SKILL: RESEARCH REPORT

Making an Outline

Organize the information from your notes in an outline. **Main topics** are the main ideas that are based on the questions you wrote. They are placed after Roman numerals. **Subtopics** are the facts that support the main topics. They are placed after capital letters. **Details** are specific facts or examples that tell about the subtopics. They are placed after numbers.

Use these notes to complete the outline below. Turn the questions into main topics. Write the supporting facts as subtopics. Write the facts that tell about the subtopics as details.

What kinds of foods will be on a space shuttle?
—dehydrated foods
—dehydrated foods such as fruits, vegetables, cereals
—canned foods

What is a description of the space suit worn outside the shuttle?
—inflatable basic layer to maintain pressure
—restraint layer to keep basic layer from ballooning
—fireproof layers for protection
—built-in backpack containing necessities

Life in a Space Shuttle

I. _____

   A. _____

      1. _____

      2. _____

      3. _____

   B. _____

II. _____

   A. _____

   B. _____

   C. _____

   D. _____

Level 8 Unit 12 Research Report *(Use with pupil book pages 439–440.)*
Skill: Students will complete an outline from notes.

Houghton Mifflin English 8
Copyright © Houghton Mifflin Company. All rights reserved.

Name _____

COMPOSITION SKILL: RESEARCH REPORT

RETEACHING WORKBOOK 93

Writing Introductions and Conclusions

> Begin every report with an **introduction** and end it with a **conclusion**. Write an introduction that captures your reader's interest. Include a sentence that tells exactly what the report is about. Write a conclusion that restates the main ideas and may also review the main points. For a short report, the introduction and conclusion are usually a paragraph each.

Read the following short report. Then rewrite the introductory paragraph and the concluding paragraph so that each one is better.

Bees can communicate with each other. I am going to tell you how they do it. It's really interesting.

Through various "dances" a bee can tell other bees the precise direction and distance of food from the hive. The circle dance tells that the food is within a hundred yards. The waggle dance, in which the bee moves in a figure eight, tells that the food is farther away. The speed of the waggle dance indicates how much farther. The faster the bee dances, the closer the food is to the hive.

During the waggle dance, the dancer indicates in which direction the bees must fly to find the food. The dancer crosses from one loop of the eight to the other in the direction of the food.

This is how bees communicate. It's kind of amazing, really, when you think about it.

Introduction: _____

_____

_____

_____

_____

_____

Conclusion: _____

_____

_____

_____

_____

_____

Houghton Mifflin English 8
Copyright © Houghton Mifflin Company. All rights reserved.

Level 8   Unit 12   **Research Report**   *(Use with pupil book pages 440–441.)*
Skill: Students will rewrite the introduction and the conclusion of a report.

Name _____ **RETEACHING WORKBOOK** **94**

COMPOSITION SKILL: RESEARCH REPORT

Making Transitions

When you write, connect sentences and paragraphs with transition words and phrases. Use transition words and phrases in the following ways.

To introduce examples: for example, for instance, to illustrate, in fact
To add another point: in addition, also, furthermore, a second
To show time relationships: finally, before, after, then, eventually
To signal results or effects: as a result, therefore, for this reason
To show comparison or contrast: similarly, just as, on the other hand
To connect ideas: yet, however, though, so, nevertheless, moreover

In each pair of sentences below, a transition word or phrase is missing. Decide what purpose the transition should have in each pair of sentences. Then write the appropriate word or phrase from those given in parentheses.

1. Space probes have analyzed the soil and atmosphere of other planets.

    _____ , scientists still have no definite proof of other living things in the solar system. **(Finally, However)**

2. The United States is "home" to some of the world's most popular sports.

    _____ , basketball was invented in Springfield, Massachusetts. **(For example, After)**

3. The athlete trained hard for years. _____ , her work paid off. **(Just as, Eventually)**

4. Bees help to pollinate flowers. _____ , they provide honey. **(On the other hand, In addition)**

5. Henry Ford figured out how to make automobiles less expensive.

    _____ , more people could afford them.
    (As a result, Before)

6. People in the United States eat beef frequently. _____ , the Japanese often eat fish. **(In contrast, Though)**

7. George Washington led the Continental Army. _____ , he served as our first President. **(For instance, In addition)**

8. Scientists are continually seeking a cure for cancer. _____ progress has been made, no cure has been found yet. **(Though, However)**

Level 8 Unit 12 Research Report *(Use with pupil book pages 442–445.)*
Skill: Students will choose appropriate transition words or phrases to connect sentences in pairs.

Houghton Mifflin English 8
Copyright © Houghton Mifflin Company. All rights reserved.

Name _____

RETEACHING WORKBOOK **95**

THE WRITING PROCESS: RESEARCH REPORT

Step 4: Revise

Have I	**yes**
replaced the dull introduction with an interesting one?	☐
added transition words and phrases?	☐
added details and clarified any confusing pronouns?	☐
crossed out a sentence that gives an opinion?	☐

Revise the following beginning of a research report. Use the check list above to help you. Check off each box when you have finished your revision.
- Use the space above each line and on the sides of the paragraphs for your changes.
- Use the outline section below to check that all the facts have been used in the report.

> **I.** How Jumbo came to the United States—1882
>   **A.** P. T. Barnum offered to buy from London Zoo
>   **1.** Largest elephant in captivity
>   **2.** Needed special attraction for circus
>   **B.** Protest by British public
>   **1.** Children who had ridden elephant wrote letters
>   **2.** Angry newspaper editorials
>   **C.** Sale completed

I'm going to tell you where the word jumbo came from. You probably don't know. It was a huge circus elephant brought to the United States by P. T. Barnum in 1882.

He needed a special attraction for his circus. He offered to buy it from the zoo. The British public strongly protested. Children who had ridden on it wrote letters. I certainly don't blame them. Newspaper editors wrote angry editorials. The sale was completed.

Houghton Mifflin English 8
Copyright © Houghton Mifflin Company. All rights reserved.

Level 8 Unit 12 Research Report *(Use with pupil book pages 451–452.)*
Skill: Students will revise part of a research report, writing an interesting introduction, adding transition words, phrases, details, and clarifying pronouns, and crossing out a sentence that gives an opinion.

Name _____

RETEACHING WORKBOOK 96

THE WRITING PROCESS: RESEARCH REPORT

Step 5: Proofread

When you proofread, look for mistakes in spelling, capitalization, punctuation, paragraph format, and grammar. Use proofreading marks to make corrections.

If you read ~~you're~~ *your* Essay to us, maybe we can learn from ~~them~~ *it*

Proofreading Marks				
⁋ Indent.	⋏ Add a comma.	⊙ Add a period.	≡ Capitalize.	Add quotation marks.
∧ Add something.	∼ Reverse the order.	Take out.	/ Make a small letter.	

Proofread these paragraphs from a report. There are four capitalization errors, four punctuation errors, two run-on sentences, one spelling error, and one mistake in paragraph format. There are three pronoun errors. Correct these errors. Use a dictionary to check your spelling.

    The constellations you see depend on the season and they also depend on where you are different constellations appear in the Northern and Southern Hemispheres. The best-known constellation in the Northern Hemisphere is the big Dipper. Two stars in this constellation point to the North Star, If you watch the big Dipper all night, it seems to move around the North Star in a circle however, the stars are not truely moving. Us earthlings are moving.

Some other constellations are the Big Bear and orion the Hunter. The Big Bear no longer looks like an animal because some stars have changed they're positions since it was named Orion is easy to spot in the winter. you will see three bright stars in a row. They are Orion's belt. Its hard to miss

Level 8 Unit 12 **Research Report** *(Use with pupil book pages 453–454.)*
Skill: Students will proofread paragraphs from a report, correcting mistakes in spelling, capitalization, punctuation, paragraph format, and grammar.

Name _____

LANGUAGE AND USAGE

RETEACHING WORKBOOK 97

1 | Prepositions and Prepositional Phrases

> ▶ A **preposition** shows the relationship between a noun or a pronoun and another word in the sentence.
>
> ▶ A **prepositional phrase** includes a preposition, the object or objects of the preposition, and all the modifiers of the object.
>
> ▶ When a pronoun is the object of a preposition, use the objective case.
>
>   preposition   object
>   Beethoven was one **of** the world's greatest **composers**.
>   prepositional phrase
>
>   preposition object object
>   **Between you** and **me**, I like his symphonies best.
>   prepositional phrase

Write the prepositional phrases in these sentences.

Example: Beethoven also performed in concerts. _____ **in concerts** _____

1. Beethoven was born in Germany during the eighteenth century.

   _____

2. We studied scores by him and several other composers of that time.

   _____

3. Because of his deafness, Beethoven stopped performing.

   _____

4. Beethoven broke new ground as a composer. _____

5. He wrote several extraordinary sonatas for the piano. _____

6. He wrote his most famous symphony toward the end of his life.

   _____

7. Beethoven studied the works of Mozart, Haydn, and other masters.

   _____

8. Beethoven created new forms in place of old ones.

   _____

Level 8 Unit 13 Phrases   *(Use with pupil book pages 462–464.)*
Skill: Students will identify prepositional phrases.

Houghton Mifflin English 8
Copyright © Houghton Mifflin Company. All rights reserved.

UNIT 13 PHRASES

Name _____

RETEACHING WORKBOOK 98

LANGUAGE AND USAGE

2 | Prepositional Phrases as Modifiers

> ▶ Prepositional phrases always function as modifiers.
> ▶ **Adjective phrases** modify nouns or pronouns.
> ▶ **Adverb phrases** modify verbs, adjectives, or adverbs.
>
> **Adjective Phrase:** The exhibit **at the museum** interested the class.
> **Adverb Phrase:** Our class traveled **to the Metropolitan Museum**.

Write each underlined adjective or adverb phrase and the word that it modifies.

Example: The bus arrived at the museum in the morning.

at the museum, in the morning—arrived

1. People of all ages visit the Metropolitan Museum.

   _____

2. The students walked into the museum.

   _____

3. They saw an exhibit of several Renaissance paintings.

   _____

4. For ten minutes Julie observed with special interest one painting.

   _____

5. Paintings by Leonardo da Vinci were hung in the special exhibit.

   _____

6. David could not see enough of the impressionistic paintings.

   _____

7. One of van Gogh's paintings especially fascinated Alex.

   _____

8. The students were interested in several of the painters.

   _____

Level 8 Unit 13 **Phrases**   (Use with pupil book pages 465–466.)
Skill: Students will identify the words modified by adjective and adverb phrases.

Houghton Mifflin English 8
Copyright © Houghton Mifflin Company. All rights reserved.

Name _____

RETEACHING WORKBOOK **99**

LANGUAGE AND USAGE

3 | Choosing the Right Preposition

> ▶ Use **between** with two people, things, or groups.
> ▶ Use **among** with more than two people, things, or groups.
> ▶ Use **beside** to mean "next to."
> ▶ Use **besides** to mean "in addition to."
>
> The director stood **between** the two characters on-stage.
> **Among** playwrights Shakespeare is perhaps the most famous.
> Several attendants sat **beside** the king.
> **Besides** the fool Cordelia remained faithful to King Lear.

Rewrite each sentence, using the correct preposition in parentheses.

Example: (Among, Between) *Hamlet* and *Macbeth*, we chose to see *Hamlet*.

Between <u>Hamlet</u> and <u>Macbeth</u>, we chose to see <u>Hamlet</u>.

1. *Hamlet* is (among, between) Shakespeare's best plays.

   _____

2. (Beside, Besides) a wonderful plot, the play has great dialogue.

   _____

3. On the way to the play, I sat (beside, besides) Jennifer.

   _____

4. We had memorized a dialogue (among, between) Hamlet and his mother.

   _____

5. Sitting (among, between) our classmates, we acted out that dialogue.

   _____

6. We acted out two other dialogues (beside, besides) that one.

   _____

7. (Among, Between) the two of us, we forgot several lines.

   _____

8. Finally, our bus arrived and parked (beside, besides) the theater.

   _____

Level 8 Unit 13 Phrases *(Use with pupil book pages 467–468.)*
Skill: Students will use the prepositions *between, among, beside,* and *besides* correctly.

Name _____ **RETEACHING WORKBOOK** 100

LANGUAGE AND USAGE

Verbals: Participles

> ▸ A **verbal** is a word that is formed from a verb. Verbals are used as nouns, adjectives, or adverbs.
> ▸ A **participle** is a verbal used as an adjective.
>
> **Blinding** lights flood the **crowded** theater.
> Those **watching** cannot guess the play's **surprising** outcome.

Write the participles that modify the underlined words in these sentences.

Example: Every year the eighth grade sees an exciting play on Broadway.
exciting

1. Experienced and prepared, the actors always give a superb performance.

   _____

2. Those seated enjoy an unobstructed view of the stage.

   _____

3. Then the students take a guided tour of Manhattan.

   _____

4. Towering buildings and flashing lights are everywhere.

   _____

5. They listen to the astounding history of the Brooklyn Bridge.

   _____

6. The Chrysler Building, striking and shining, delights them.

   _____

7. Later the class enjoys an inspiring concert at Carnegie Hall.

   _____

8. Then the students, exhausted and worn, return home by train.

   _____

Level 8 Unit 13 Phrases   (Use with pupil book pages 469–470.)
Skill: Students will identify participles.

Name _____

LANGUAGE AND USAGE

5 | Participial Phrases

RETEACHING WORKBOOK 101

> ▶ A **participial phrase** is a participle and its accompanying words.
> ▶ Participial phrases may contain direct objects, prepositional phrases, and adverbs.
>
> **Reading about the subject first,** Ann wrote about Thomas Jefferson.

Write the participial phrase in each sentence.

Example: Raised in Virginia, Jefferson later became its governor.
Raised in Virginia

1. Studying law in Virginia, Thomas Jefferson heard Patrick Henry speak.

2. Jefferson, elected to the House of Burgesses, served faithfully.

3. Being an excellent architect, he designed his home, Monticello.

4. Rejecting British views, Jefferson insisted on a colonial government.

5. Writing for the Continental Congress, he drafted the Declaration of Independence.

6. Making few changes, the Congress adopted the Declaration.

7. Jefferson, admired by many, became Vice President.

8. Inaugurated in Washington, Jefferson later became the third President.

Level 8   Unit 13   Phrases   (Use with pupil book pages 471–472.)
Skill: Students will identify participial phrases.

Name _____ RETEACHING WORKBOOK 102

LANGUAGE AND USAGE

6 | Verbals: Gerunds

> ▶ A **gerund** is the present participle of a verb used as a noun.
> ▶ A gerund functions in all of the ways that a noun does.
>
> **Subject:** **Jogging** is my favorite sport.
> **Direct Object:** I like **jogging**.
> **Object of Preposition:** Now is a good time for **jogging**.
> **Predicate Noun:** My favorite sport is **jogging**.

Write the gerunds in these sentences. Write *none* if a sentence does not have a gerund.

Example: In the spring and summer, Sharon enjoys canoeing.

canoeing

1. Hiking is Fred's favorite summer activity.

2. Golf and tennis are good ways of relaxing.

3. Terry goes to a nearby rink and teaches skating.

4. Running is a convenient sport for many people.

5. A sport that takes courage and skill is skiing.

6. At the community pool, Nancy practices diving and swimming.

7. Tim and Denise have a running argument about spectator sports.

8. Gloria's favorite spectator sport is sailing.

Level 8 Unit 13 Phrases   (Use with pupil book pages 473–474.)
Skill: Students will identify gerunds.

Name _____

RETEACHING WORKBOOK

LANGUAGE AND USAGE

7 | Gerund Phrases

> ▶ A **gerund phrase** can be a subject, a direct object, an object of a preposition, or a predicate noun.
> ▶ Use a possessive noun or a possessive pronoun before a gerund.
>
> **Subject: Thinking of a story** takes effort.
> **Direct Object:** Tom began **his thinking about a plot**.
> **Object of Preposition:** Before **starting his story,** he read others.
> **Predicate Noun:** Tom's difficulty was **creating a setting**.

A. Write each gerund phrase and underline the gerund.

Example: Creating a believable story took some time.
<u>Creating</u> a believable story

1. Describing the main character was easy for Tom.

_____

2. Tom began outlining a very rough plot.

_____

3. After writing the first few paragraphs, Tom stopped.

_____

B. Write each sentence, using the correct possessive noun or pronoun in parentheses.

Example: (Tom, Tom's) writing a novel might earn him some fame.
Tom's writing a novel might earn him some fame.

4. He listened to (our, us) discussing the plot.

_____

5. He did not like (Sarah, Sarah's) retelling of the story.

_____

6. A (reviewer's, reviewer) criticizing the story did not hurt his feelings.

_____

Level 8 Unit 13 Phrases   *(Use with pupil book pages 475–477.)*
Skill: Students will identify gerund phrases and will use possessive nouns or possessive pronouns in gerund phrases.

Name _____ RETEACHING WORKBOOK **104**

LANGUAGE AND USAGE

8 | Verbals: Infinitives

> ▶ An **infinitive** is formed with the word *to* and the base form of the verb.
> ▶ An infinitive can be used as a noun, an adjective, or an adverb.
>
> **Noun:** Dana likes **to read**.
> **Adjective:** Novels are good books **to read**.
> **Adverb:** Most newspapers are easy **to read**.

Write the infinitives in these sentences. Write *none* if the sentence does not have an infinitive.

Example: A good book can be a way to explore.   _to explore_

1. To communicate is the aim of most authors. _____

2. To read is a way to grow. _____

3. A long novel is not necessarily a hard one to follow. _____

4. Lending a good book to a friend can be very satisfying. _____

5. If you want nothing except to escape, read a fantasy adventure. _____

6. If you want to learn, read a more serious book. _____

7. Whether a book is light or serious, read to understand. _____

8. For some books a quick way to read is to skim. _____

9. If you are willing to concentrate, a difficult book is worthwhile. _____

10. Some books are good enough to reread. _____

Level 8 Unit 13 Phrases   (*Use with pupil book pages 478–479.*)
Skill: Students will identify infinitives.

Name _____

RETEACHING WORKBOOK

LANGUAGE AND USAGE

 Infinitive Phrases

> ▶ An **infinitive phrase** consists of an infinitive and words that complete its meaning.
> ▶ An infinitive phrase acts as a noun, an adjective, or an adverb.
>   **Noun:** **To ask for money and ships** took courage.
>   **Adjective:** Columbus was the first person **to attempt the voyage**.
>   **Adverb:** He was eager **to reach the Far East**.

Write the infinitive phrase in each sentence.

Example: To make the voyage, Columbus needed ships and supplies.
   To make the voyage

1. The first task was to ask a king or queen for the funds. _____

2. Most rulers were not prepared to take such a risk. _____

3. Like most explorers Columbus was not one to accept defeat. _____

4. To find an easy route to rich islands was his goal. _____

5. Explorers sailed to gain wealth and fame. _____

6. They wanted to explore new worlds. _____

7. The explorers were brave to face the unknown. _____

8. They did not have accurate maps to guide them safely. _____

9. Some explorers were not sturdy enough to survive the hardships. _____

10. Others lived to enjoy the glory of their discoveries. _____

Level 8   Unit 13   Phrases   (Use with pupil book pages 480–481.)
Skill: Students will identify infinitive phrases.

Name _____   **RETEACHING WORKBOOK** **106**

LANGUAGE AND USAGE

10 | Combining Sentences: Phrases

> ► You can combine sentences by using prepositional phrases, participial phrases, gerund phrases, or infinitive phrases.
>
> **Two Sentences:** I read that book. It is by Charles Dickens.
> **Prepositional Phrase:** I read that book **by Charles Dickens**.
> **Two Sentences:** Bob Cratchit was a bookkeeper. Scrooge employed him.
> **Participial Phrase:** Bob Cratchit was a bookkeeper **employed by Scrooge**.
> **Two Sentences:** Bob Cratchit carried Tiny Tim. Cratchit enjoyed it.
> **Gerund Phrase:** Bob Cratchit enjoyed **carrying Tiny Tim**.
> **Two Sentences:** Cratchit needed more money. It would help Tiny Tim.
> **Infinitive Phrase:** Cratchit needed more money **to help Tiny Tim**.

Use the kind of phrase named in parentheses to combine each pair of sentences.

Example: The story takes place long ago. It takes place in London.   **(prepositional)**

The story takes place long ago in London.

1.   Cratchit worked hard. He did it to support his family.   **(infinitive)**

_____

2.   Scrooge clung to his money. This was his only pleasure.   **(gerund)**

_____

3.   Scrooge had dreams. They were about his past, present, and future.
(prepositional)

_____

4.   Marley appeared in Scrooge's dreams. He brought Scrooge a warning.
(infinitive)

_____

5.   Scrooge decided to change. He was scared by his dreams.   **(participial)**

_____

6.   Scrooge arrived at the Cratchits'. He was carrying gifts.   **(participial)**

_____

Level 8   Unit 13   Phrases   *(Use with pupil book pages 482–483.)*
Skill: Students will combine sentences, using four kinds of phrases.

Name _____

RETEACHING WORKBOOK **107**

LANGUAGE AND USAGE

1 | Independent and Subordinate Clauses

> ► A **clause** is a group of words that has a subject and a predicate.
> ► An **independent clause** expresses a complete thought.
> ► A **subordinate clause** does not state a complete thought and cannot stand alone as a sentence.
>
> | **Phrase** | **Clause** |
> |---|---|
> | | subject predicate |
> | **after** many cold days | **after** the weather turned cold |
> | **Independent Clause** | **Subordinate Clause** |
> | the ground hardens | **when** the ground hardens |

A. Label each clause *independent* or *subordinate*.

Example: when the weather gets cold enough   subordinate

1. the snow falls steadily _____

2. the wind blows through the leafless trees _____

3. before the winter begins _____

4. while the deer look for food in the snow _____

5. the wind finally dies down _____

B. Label each group of words *phrase* or *clause*.

Example: before the cold weather comes   clause

6. as the sky clears _____

7. since the first snowfall _____

8. before winter actually begins _____

9. since winter is approaching _____

10. until a heavy snowstorm _____

11. after people shovel their walks _____

12. after weeks of low temperatures _____

13. until the lake freezes _____

14. before the end of February _____

Level 8 Unit 14 Clauses   *(Use with pupil book pages 502–503.)*
Skill: Students will identify phrases, independent clauses, and subordinate clauses.

Houghton Mifflin English 8
Copyright © Houghton Mifflin Company. All rights reserved.

UNIT 14 CLAUSES

Name _____

RETEACHING WORKBOOK **108**

LANGUAGE AND USAGE

2 | Adjective Clauses

> ► An **adjective clause** modifies a noun or a pronoun.
> ► A **relative pronoun** such as *who, which,* or *that* usually introduces an adjective clause.
> ► The words *where* and *when* also introduce adjective clauses.
>
> The woman **who cares for the cats** gives them milk.
> My cat, **which was a stray cat,** is now a good house pet.
> The cat **that Tom owns** is a special breed.

Write the adjective clause in each sentence.

Example: The house cat, which is related to wild cats, is quite tame.

which is related to wild cats _____

1. The amount of food that a cat needs depends on its age and size.

   _____

2. Those who own cats soon learn their pets' likes and dislikes.

   _____

3. Cats usually like dairy products, which are good for them.

   _____

4. The joints that cats have give them agility.

   _____

5. Cats' paws, which are cushioned by pads, enable them to move quietly.

   _____

6. The time when a cat's vision is best is at night.

   _____

7. Scientists who study cats are also interested in their vocal cords.

   _____

8. The sounds that a cat makes include purring and growling.

   _____

Level 8 Unit 14 **Clauses**   *(Use with pupil book pages 504–505.)*
Skill: Students will identify adjective clauses.

Name _____

RETEACHING WORKBOOK 109

LANGUAGE AND USAGE

3 | Adjective Clauses with *who, whom,* and *whose*

▶ Use **who** when the relative pronoun is the subject of the adjective clause.
▶ Use **whom** when the relative pronoun is the direct object or the object of a preposition in the adjective clause.
▶ Use **whose** when the relative pronoun shows possession.

Subject: Frost is a poet **who** often wrote about New England.
Direct Object: Frost is a poet **whom** many people admire.
Object of Preposition: Frost is a poet for **whom** I have great respect.
Possessive Pronoun: Frost is a poet **whose** poems are widely read today.

Write each sentence, using the correct relative pronoun in parentheses.

Example: Our teacher, (who, whom) admires Frost, read his poems.

Our teacher, who admires Frost, read his poems.

1. Frost was a poet (who, whose) was often optimistic about people.

   _____

2. He was a poet (who, whose) words touched many readers.

   _____

3. Frost, (who, whose) poems contain insight, wrote about human nature.

   _____

4. The poet, (who, whom) critics still study today, wrote about New England.

   _____

5. Frost, (whom, who) was born in San Francisco, moved to New England.

   _____

6. The characters about (who, whom) he wrote live today in his poems.

   _____

7. The poet, (whose, who) was also a farmer, created images of rural life.

   _____

8. Farmers, with (whose, whom) Frost identified, often speak in his poems.

   _____

Level 8 Unit 14 Clauses *(Use with pupil book pages 506–507.)*
Skill: Students will use *who, whom,* and *whose* correctly.

Name _____

RETEACHING WORKBOOK 110

LANGUAGE AND USAGE

 Essential and Nonessential Clauses

> ▶ An adjective clause is either essential or nonessential.
> ▶ An **essential clause** identifies the noun or the pronoun modified. It is not set off by commas.
> ▶ A **nonessential clause** gives extra information about the noun or the pronoun it modifies. It is set off by commas.
> **Essential Clause:** Anyone **who visits St. Louis** will like it.
> **Nonessential Clause:** Missouri, **which has many farms,** is quite pretty.

Write each adjective clause. Label each clause *essential* or *nonessential*.

Example: Mark Twain, who was a famous novelist, came from Missouri.
<u>who was a famous novelist—nonessential</u>

1. Missouri, which is a colorful state, is in the Midwest.

2. The arch that is in St. Louis looks impressive.

3. St. Louis and Kansas City, which are both in Missouri, are large cities.

4. Trails that were crucial to western expansion began in Missouri.

5. Lewis and Clark, who explored the West, set out from St. Louis.

6. Those who traveled the Mississippi usually rode on steamboats.

7. Harry Truman, who was born in Missouri, was the state's most famous politician.

8. A famous scientist who came from Missouri was George Washington Carver.

Level 8 Unit 14 Clauses *(Use with pupil book pages 508–509.)*
Skill: Students will identify essential and nonessential clauses.

Name _____ **RETEACHING WORKBOOK** **111**

LANGUAGE AND USAGE

5 | Adverb Clauses

> ▸ An **adverb clause** is a subordinate clause used as an adverb.
> ▸ A **subordinating conjunction** introduces an adverb clause.
> ▸ Use a comma after an adverb clause that begins a sentence.
>
> **While we were in Canada**, we toured Montreal.   (modifies verb *toured*)
> It was larger **than we expected**.   (modifies the adjective *larger*)
> I thought about that trip long **after I returned**.   (modifies the adverb *long*)

Write each adverb clause and the word or words that it modifies.

Example: We traveled to Montreal even though it was raining.

　　　　　even though it was raining—traveled

1. Whenever I see a map of Canada, I think of our trip to Montreal.

   _____

2. We reached the border after we traveled through New York State.

   _____

3. Wherever we went, the people in Montreal greeted us pleasantly.

   _____

4. We were delighted when we saw the botanical gardens.

   _____

5. If you visit Montreal, see Mount Royal Park.

   _____

6. It is colder in Montreal than it is in most of the United States.

   _____

7. Before we visited the shops in Montreal, we saw several churches.

   _____

8. We enjoyed the visit more than we had expected.

   _____

Level 8 Unit 14 Clauses   *(Use with pupil book pages 510–512.)*
Skill: Students will identify adverb clauses and the words that they modify.

Name _____

RETEACHING WORKBOOK 112

LANGUAGE AND USAGE

Noun Clauses

> ▶ A **noun clause** is a subordinate clause that acts as a noun.
> ▶ Use *who* and *whoever* as subjects in noun clauses.
> ▶ Use *whom* and *whomever* as objects in noun clauses.
>
> **Subject:** **What is wrong with the car** is a mystery.
> **Direct Object:** I do not know **what the matter is**.
> **Indirect Object:** Give **whoever does the repairs** the keys.
> **Object of Preposition:** I am prepared for **whatever must be done**.
> **Predicate Noun:** A complete tune-up is **what the car needs**.

A. Write the noun clause in each sentence.

Example: Whoever did these repairs did a good job.

Whoever did these repairs

1. Gasoline, air, and electricity are what turns the car's engine.

   _____

2. A mechanic knows how the engine works.

   _____

3. The carburetor mixes air with whatever fuels the car.

   _____

4. That the carburetor needed adjustment was apparent.

   _____

B. Rewrite each sentence, using the correct relative pronoun in parentheses.

Example: Tell me (who, whom) is the best mechanic.

Tell me who is the best mechanic.

5. (Whoever, Whomever) repairs cars must understand how they work.

   _____

6. (Whoever, Whomever) you call should be able to answer your questions.

   _____

Level 8 Unit 14 Clauses   *(Use with pupil book pages 513–515.)*
Skill: Students will identify noun clauses and will use relative pronouns correctly.

Name _____

LANGUAGE AND USAGE

RETEACHING WORKBOOK 113

Combining Sentences: Subordinate Clauses

▶ You can use subordinate clauses to combine sentences with related ideas into a single complex sentence.

Two Sentences: New York is an exciting place. Most visitors think so.
Noun Clause: Most visitors think **that New York is an exciting place**.
Two Sentences: Joan took a trip to New York. She enjoyed it.
Adjective Clause: Joan took a trip to New York, **which she enjoyed**.
Two Sentences: Joan liked New York. She hoped to return.
Adverb Clause: Because Joan liked New York, she hoped to return.

Combine each pair of simple sentences into a complex sentence, using the type of clause and the conjunction shown in parentheses. Use commas where they are needed.

Example: We went to New York. We wanted to see skyscrapers.
   (adverb—because)
   We went to New York because we wanted to see skyscrapers.

1. We learned about New York. It was interesting. **(noun—what)**

   _____

2. President Roosevelt was once governor of New York. It came as a surprise to some of us. **(noun—that)**

   _____

   _____

3. We admired Albany's skyline. We crossed the Hudson River. **(adverb—as)**

   _____

4. We visited the Eastman House. It is in Rochester. **(adjective—which)**

   _____

5. New York City is fascinating. You can also see exciting things in other parts of the state. **(adverb—although)**

   _____

   _____

Level 8   Unit 14   Clauses   *(Use with pupil book pages 516–517.)*
Skill: Students will combine sentences, using subordinate clauses.

Teacher's Annotated Pages

Name _____

RETEACHING WORKBOOK

LANGUAGE AND USAGE

1 Kinds of Sentences

▶ A **declarative** sentence makes a statement and ends with a period.
▶ An **interrogative** sentence asks a question and ends with a question mark.
▶ An **imperative** sentence makes a command or a request and ends with a period.
▶ An **exclamatory** sentence shows strong feeling and ends with an exclamation point.

Declarative: Stephen Foster was an American songwriter.
Interrogative: Did you know he was born on the Fourth of July?
Imperative: Please sing a medley of his songs. Don't refuse.
Exclamatory: Aren't his songs beautiful! Foster was talented!

Label each sentence *declarative, interrogative, imperative,* or *exclamatory.*

Example: When did Stephen Foster live?   **interrogative**

1. Stephen Foster lived from 1826 to 1864. **declarative**
2. He had no formal education in music. **declarative**
3. Why did he start writing music? **interrogative**
4. He simply fell in love with it! **exclamatory**
5. Stephen began writing songs as a child. **declarative**
6. Isn't "Old Folks at Home" great! **exclamatory**
7. Do you know who the composer is? **interrogative**
8. It must be Stephen Foster. **declarative**
9. Don't forget the well-known "Oh! Susanna." **imperative**
10. Was it written by Foster too? **interrogative**
11. Did the song become popular quickly? **interrogative**
12. Please tell me something about that funny song. **imperative**
13. Foster composed it at the young age of twenty! **exclamatory**
14. Tell me more. **imperative**
15. "Oh! Susanna" and another song earned him $10,000! **exclamatory**

Level 8   Unit 1   The Sentence   (Use with pupil book pages 14–15.)
Skill: Students will identify the four kinds of sentences.

Name _____

RETEACHING WORKBOOK

LANGUAGE AND USAGE

2 Complete Subjects and Complete Predicates

▶ The **complete subject** names *whom* or *what* the sentence is about.
▶ The **complete predicate** tells what the subject *is, does, has,* or *feels.*

Complete Subjects	Complete Predicates
The Florio family	traveled to Italy last summer.
They	visited many relatives.
John and Gina Florio	toured.

Write the underlined words. Then label them *complete subject* or *complete predicate.*

Example: Italy is in southern Europe.
Italy—complete subject
is in southern Europe—complete predicate

1. Italy consists of a peninsula and two islands. **Italy—complete subject**
2. Much of Italy has a pleasant Mediterranean climate. **has a pleasant Mediterranean climate—complete predicate**
3. The capital of Italy is Rome. **is Rome—complete predicate**
4. The city has existed for more than two thousand years. **has existed for more than two thousand years—complete predicate**
5. It has earned the name the Eternal City. **It—complete subject**
6. The Roman Empire was established by Augustus. **The Roman Empire—complete subject**
7. Half of the people in Italy live in cities today. **live in cities today—complete predicate**
8. Most industries are in the northern part of the country. **Most industries—complete subject**
9. Many people are farmers. **are farmers—complete predicate**
10. People on the coast fish for a living. **People on the coast—complete subject**

Level 8   Unit 1   The Sentence   (Use with pupil book pages 16–17.)
Skill: Students will identify complete subjects and complete predicates.

T1

Name _____

LANGUAGE AND USAGE   RETEACHING WORKBOOK (3)

3 | Simple Subjects and Simple Predicates

▶ The **simple subject** is the key word or words in the complete subject.
▶ The **simple predicate** is the key word or words in the complete predicate.

Subjects	Predicates
People	**eat** rice as their main food.
This important **crop**	is **grown** widely in Asia.
Other **types** of crops	have not **become** as popular.

Write the underlined words. Then label them *simple subject* or *simple predicate*.

Example: Rice plants <u>grow</u> to about four feet high.
grow—simple predicate

1. Many farmers <u>plant</u> rice in low-lying fields.
plant—simple predicate

2. <u>They</u> grow many different kinds of rice.   They—simple subject

3. Heavy rainfall <u>helps</u>.   helps—simple predicate

4. A <u>grain</u> of rice has a tough outer covering.
grain—simple subject

5. People <u>do</u> not <u>eat</u> the hull.   do eat—simple predicate

6. A layer of bran <u>covers</u> the rice kernel.
covers—simple predicate

7. <u>Asia</u> produces most of the world's rice.
Asia—simple subject

8. The <u>United States</u> is also a major producer.
United States—simple subject

9. <u>Millions</u> of people live chiefly on rice.
Millions—simple subject

10. The popularity of rice <u>is increasing</u>.
is increasing—simple predicate

Level 8 Unit 1 The Sentence   (Use with pupil book pages 18–19.)
Skill: Students will identify simple subjects and simple predicates.

Name _____

LANGUAGE AND USAGE   RETEACHING WORKBOOK (4)

4 | Finding the Subject

▶ To find the subject of a sentence in **inverted order**, put the subject and the predicate in **natural order**.

Inverted Order	Natural Order
Out of nowhere came **lightning**.	**Lightning** came out of nowhere.
Here comes the **storm**.	The **storm** comes here.
Is **everybody** safe?	**Everybody** is safe.

▶ The **subject** of an imperative sentence is always *you* understood.
(You) Stand by the side. (You) Please wait.

Write the simple subject of each sentence. If the subject is *you* understood, write (You).

Example: Down the street rushes a crowd of people.   crowd

1. There is a loud clap of thunder.   clap
2. Across the sky lightning flashes.   lightning
3. Down pours the rain.   rain
4. Where can we go to stay dry?   we
5. When will the storm end?   storm
6. Here is a place with umbrellas for sale.   place
7. Go into the shop quickly.   (You)
8. Buy two large umbrellas.   (You)
9. Inside the shop are about one hundred people!   people
10. Don't go back out into the storm.   (You)
11. Please stay in here.   (You)
12. On the wall near the back door is a telephone.   telephone
13. Here is some change.   change
14. Call home immediately.   (You)

Level 8 Unit 1 The Sentence   (Use with pupil book pages 20–21.)
Skill: Students will identify simple subjects in inverted and in imperative sentences.

Name _____

RETEACHING WORKBOOK

6 Combining Sentences: Compound Sentences

LANGUAGE AND USAGE

▶ You can combine two or more related sentences into a **compound sentence**. Join the sentences with a conjunction. Add a comma before the conjunction.

Simple Sentences: Foxes are wild animals. Some live in big cities.
Compound Sentence: Foxes are wild animals, **but** some live in big cities.
Simple Sentences: Can you approach a fox? Is it too dangerous?
Compound Sentence: Can you approach a fox, **or** is it too dangerous?

Write each pair of sentences as one compound sentence. Use the conjunction in parentheses, and add a comma where needed.

Example: Foxes are clever animals. They are skillful hunters. (and)
Foxes are clever animals, and they are skillful hunters.

1. Foxes are related to wolves. They are smarter than wolves. (but)
   Foxes are related to wolves, but they are smarter than wolves.

2. A female fox is a vixen. A young fox is called a pup. (and)
   A female fox is a vixen, and a young fox is called a pup.

3. A baby fox needs its parents' care. It will not survive. (or)
   A baby fox needs its parents' care, or it will not survive.

4. Foxes play an important role. Farmers depend on them. (and)
   Foxes play an important role, and farmers depend on them.

5. Foxes eat mice. Mice eat farmers' crops. (and)
   Foxes eat mice, and mice eat farmers' crops.

6. The red fox lives mainly on rodents. It will eat anything. (but)
   The red fox lives mainly on rodents, but it will eat anything.

7. Have you seen a fox in the woods? Have you just seen pictures? (or)
   Have you seen a fox in the woods, or have you just seen pictures?

8. A fox may look like a dog. Never mix up the two! (but)
   A fox may look like a dog, but never mix up the two!

Level 8 Unit 1 The Sentence   (Use with pupil book pages 24–25.)
Skill: Students will form compound sentences.

Name _____

RETEACHING WORKBOOK

5 Compound Subjects and Compound Predicates

LANGUAGE AND USAGE

▶ A **compound subject** is made up of two or more simple subjects.
▶ A **compound predicate** is made up of two or more simple predicates.

Compound Subject: **People, animals,** and **plants** inhabit the earth.
Compound Predicate: Do they **live, grow,** and **thrive** everywhere?

Write the simple subjects or simple predicates that are joined by each underlined conjunction.

Example: Scientists have discovered and named many kinds of animals.
have discovered, named

1. No continent or ocean lacks living things. **continent, ocean**

2. Plants and animals are important to the environment.
   Plants, animals

3. Green plants provide food and give off oxygen. **provide, give**

4. Neither yeast plants nor mold plants are green, however.
   plants, plants

5. Mold seeds float in the air, settle on food, and grow into plants.
   float, settle, grow

6. Plants rely on and enrich the soil. **rely, enrich**

7. Air and water are necessary for survival. **Air, water**

8. Many scientists collect soil samples and analyze the contents.
   collect, analyze

9. Some scientists study plants but may not work outside a lab.
   study, may work

10. Do ecologists or astronomers study our environment?
    ecologists, astronomers

Level 8 Unit 1 The Sentence   (Use with pupil book pages 22–23.)
Skill: Students will identify compound subjects and compound predicates.

T3

LANGUAGE AND USAGE

7 | Conjunctions

> ▶ **Coordinating conjunctions** join words or groups of words.
> ▶ **Correlative conjunctions** are used in pairs to join words or groups of words.
>
> **Coordinating Conjunctions:** and, but, or, nor, for, yet
> **Correlative Conjunctions:** either . . . or   both . . . and
>   neither . . . nor   not only . . . but (also)

Write the coordinating or correlative conjunctions in each sentence.

Example: Painting is an old and important art form.   **and**

1. An artist expresses ideas or presents feelings in a personal way.   **or**

2. People paint realistic scenes or abstracts.   **or**

3. Either the first method or the second can produce a beautiful painting.   **Either . . . or**

4. Not only shapes but also colors are important in a painting.   **Not only . . . but also**

5. Both children and adults can paint.   **Both . . . and**

6. Painting is easy, but painting well is not.   **but**

7. Many artists work long hours, for they are perfectionists.   **for**

8. Some painters will not tire, nor will they give up.   **nor**

9. An artist's life is difficult yet satisfying.   **yet**

10. Neither fame nor wealth comes to many artists.   **Neither . . . nor**

11. The joy and satisfaction are what count.   **and**

12. Children and adults admire paintings in museums.   **and**

13. Museums not only have displays but also offer tours.   **not only . . . but also**

14. Visitors may ask questions or offer comments.   **or**

Level 8   Unit 1   The Sentence   (Use with pupil book pages 26–27.)
Skill: Students will identify coordinatng and correlative conjunctions.

T4

LANGUAGE AND USAGE

8 | Complex Sentences

> ▶ An **independent clause** can stand alone.
> ▶ A **subordinate clause** cannot stand alone and usually begins with a subordinating conjunction.
> ▶ A **complex sentence** has an independent clause and one or more subordinate clauses.
>
>   subordinate clause   independent clause
>   **Because they grow in all climates,** trees are found almost everywhere.
>
>   independent clause   subordinate clause
>   Trees are found almost everywhere **because they grow in all climates.**

Write the subordinate clause in each complex sentence.

Example: Whereas some trees have many uses, others are simply beautiful.
              Whereas some trees have many uses

1. There are more kinds of trees than you can imagine.
   than you can imagine

2. The odd-shaped Joshua tree grows in the desert where most plants cannot live.
   where most plants cannot live

3. Whenever people see the tree, they notice its dagger-shaped leaves.
   Whenever people see the tree

4. The flowering peach tree should have a different name since it produces no peaches.
   since it produces no peaches

5. Many people imagine otherwise because it has this misleading name.
   because it has this misleading name

6. The sausage tree sounds tasty although its fruit is not edible.
   although its fruit is not edible

7. As you might expect, the flowers of the pocket-handkerchief tree look like handkerchiefs.
   As you might expect

Name _____

RETEACHING WORKBOOK

LANGUAGE AND USAGE

10 | Interjections

▶ An interjection shows strong feeling or represents a sound. Use a comma or an exclamation point after an interjection.

Common Interjections

oh, dear	ah	hooray	well	oh, my	phew
oh, yes/no	aha	ouch	wow	ugh	shh

Wow! This is a bird watcher's paradise!
Oh, yes, there are over two hundred kinds of birds here.

Write each interjection and the punctuation mark that follows it.

Example: Oh, I like being at Yosemite National Park.   Oh,

1. Shh! I think I see a deer.   Shh!
2. Goodness, it looks like a whole family.   Goodness,
3. Well, try not to frighten them, so I can take a picture.   Well,
4. Uh oh, they are starting to run away.   Uh oh,
5. Phew! I managed to get the shot.   Phew!
6. Hooray! You're the best photographer!   Hooray!
7. Hey, let's hike to Sentinel Falls today.   Hey,
8. Okay, I ought to get some good pictures there.   Okay,
9. Oh, my! Do the falls really drop two thousand feet?   Oh, my!
10. Wow! That is quite a plunge!   Wow!
11. Good grief, I've no more film for the camera.   Good grief,
12. Ugh! What do we do now?   Ugh!
13. Aha, there's a drugstore over there.   Aha,
14. Oh, yes, I'm sure that they sell all kinds of film.   Oh, yes,
15. Bravo! We'll have great pictures after all!   Bravo!

Level 8   Unit 1   The Sentence   (Use with pupil book pages 34–35.)
Skill: Students will identify interjections.

Name _____

RETEACHING WORKBOOK

LANGUAGE AND USAGE

9 | Correcting Fragments and Run-ons

▶ A sentence fragment is an incomplete thought.
   Fragment: Is the largest country in the world.
   Sentence: The Soviet Union is the largest country in the world.

▶ A run-on sentence strings together too many thoughts without correct punctuation.
   Run-on: It has a harsh climate, many problems arise.
   Simple Sentences: It has a harsh climate. Many problems arise.
   Compound Sentence: It has a harsh climate, **and** many problems arise.
   Complex Sentence: **Because** it has a harsh climate, many problems arise.

Correct these sentence fragments and run-on sentences.

Example: Has a huge coastline.   The Soviet Union has a huge coastline.
Sample answers:

1. In the Soviet Union, cold weather.
   In the Soviet Union, cold weather sometimes creates problems.
2. The country has a long coastline, most ports are used only in warm weather.
   The country has a long coastline, but most ports are used only in warm weather.
3. Inland waterways are also a problem, many freeze in winter.
   Inland waterways are also a problem because many freeze in winter.
4. Because of bad weather, many products.
   Because of bad weather, many products are moved over land.
5. Although travel by water would be cheaper.
   Although travel by water would be cheaper, it is often impossible.
6. The country has large deposits of coal and iron, it exports steel and machinery.
   The country has large deposits of coal and iron, and it exports steel and machinery.
7. Many Soviet citizens are farmers, they grow wheat, rye, and corn.
   Many Soviet citizens are farmers. They grow wheat, rye, and corn.
8. Moscow and Leningrad the largest cities.
   Moscow and Leningrad are the largest cities in the Soviet Union.

Level 8   Unit 1   The Sentence   (Use with pupil book pages 31–33.)
Skill: Students will correct sentence fragments and run-ons.

T5

Writing a Good Beginning

Write a good beginning that will capture your readers' interest and will make them want to read on.

Poor Beginning: Someone told me to stop as I walked in the door.
Good Beginning: "Halt!" the security guard ordered, as alarms went off all around me.

Each personal narrative below needs a better beginning. Read the story. Then write a good beginning to replace the underlined sentence. Begin with an action, with dialogue, with details about the setting, or with details about yourself or another character.

The man told me that he needed help. I could see that he was breathing normally, so it was safe to leave him for a minute. I ran to a pay phone and called the emergency number. Then I rushed back to the man and introduced myself. I talked soothingly to him and tried to keep him calm. Within minutes we heard the sirens of an ambulance.

"Thank you, Gina," the injured man said as they carried him into the ambulance. "You may have saved my life."

Answers will vary.

Good Beginning: _____

_____

_____

When I looked out the window the morning after the big snowstorm, there was a lot of snow. "People are going to need some help digging out of this," I said to my little brother Don. "Grab a shovel and let's go."

School was canceled for the day, but many of our neighbors still had to get to work. We were able to dig out five driveways before breakfast. By then we'd worked up a huge appetite and earned ourselves more money than Don had ever made before. His eyes and cheeks were glowing as he wolfed down his breakfast.

Answers will vary.

Good Beginning: _____

_____

_____

_____

Supplying Details

Use details that show what a person, place, thing, or event is like.

Poor Detail: Everyone teased me when I bowled.
Good Detail: My friends groaned and shrieked when I rolled another gutter ball.

The following paragraph from a personal narrative is not very interesting. Rewrite each sentence from the paragraph, adding details to show exactly what the event was like.

I played my best game ever last night. I had trained hard for it. I started doing things right from the very beginning. Some people told me I was doing really well. I felt good afterward.

1. I played my best game ever last night.
   Answers will vary.

   _____

2. I had trained hard for it.

   _____

   _____

3. I started doing things right from the very beginning.

   _____

   _____

4. Some people told me I was doing really well.

   _____

   _____

5. I felt good afterward.

   _____

   _____

Name _____

COMPOSITION SKILL: PERSONAL NARRATIVE

RETEACHING WORKBOOK 14

Writing a Good Ending

A good ending *shows* rather than *tells* what happened. It leaves the reader with a feeling that fits the mood of the story.

Poor Ending: It turned out in the end that I won the award.
Good Ending: As I jumped out of my chair and ran up to receive the Athlete of the Year award, I couldn't help grinning from ear to ear.

Read the following closing paragraphs for personal narratives. Then write a good ending to replace the underlined sentences in each paragraph. Show rather than tell what happened.

Finally, we packed our suitcases, checked out of the hotel, and took the bus to the airport. That's how our vacation in Hawaii ended. We had had a really good time and were sad to leave.

Good Ending: _**Answers will vary.**_ _____
_____
_____

We were breathing more heavily with every step. "I don't know if I can get to the top," whispered Marge. "I can't go another step." She was really glad when I told her she didn't have to because I saw the marker that said we were actually already at the peak.

Good Ending: _**Answers will vary.**_ _____
_____
_____

Level 8 Unit 2 Personal Narrative (Use with pupil book pages 72–73.)
Skill: Students will write good endings for stories.

Name _____

COMPOSITION SKILL: PERSONAL NARRATIVE

RETEACHING WORKBOOK 13

Writing Dialogue

Use **dialogue** in a story to make the characters and action seem real.

Without Dialogue: Harriet said that she had enjoyed the science-fiction movie.
With Dialogue: "Wow! Those were the most incredible special effects I've ever seen in a science-fiction movie," Harriet said.

Imagine that each situation described below has happened to you. Write a few lines of dialogue that you could use for a personal narrative about the situation. Try to show the feelings and personality of each character in the way he or she speaks.

1. Mary whispered some encouraging words to me before I went on stage. I thanked her.
   **Answers will vary.** _____
   _____
   _____

2. Our new neighbor invited me to see her dog. I tried to get out of it. She insisted.
   _____
   _____
   _____

3. Rodney told me he had saved enough money to buy a racing bicycle at last. I was jealous but tried not to show it. I could tell that he knew anyway.
   _____
   _____
   _____

Level 8 Unit 2 Personal Narrative (Use with pupil book pages 70–71.)
Skill: Students will write dialogue for different situations.

UNIT 2 TEACHER'S ANNOTATED PAGES

Name _____

THE WRITING PROCESS: PERSONAL NARRATIVE

RETEACHING WORKBOOK 15

Step 3: Revise

Have I

	yes
written a new beginning that captures the reader's attention?	☐
crossed out dull parts and added details that *show* rather than *tell*?	☐
added dialogue that makes the characters seem real?	☐
written a new ending that fits the mood of the story and that *shows* rather than *tells*?	☐

Revise the following story. Use the check list above to help you. Check off each box when you have finished your revision.

● Use the space above each line, on the sides, and below the paragraphs for your changes.

Sample answers:

When you're accident-prone, even a shopping mall has its pitfalls.

~~I went to the mall on Saturday.~~ I was riding up an escalator

at the mall on Saturday

when the front of my sandal got caught at the top of the moving

hard   blue and white sandal

stairway. I looked down in amazement. I tugged at the ~~shoe.~~

wedged in the mechanism. My shoe

~~It~~ wouldn't come loose. I didn't know what to do.

Meanwhile, the escalator was bringing a crowd of people

an embarrassed grin on my face and with

toward me. I stepped out of the way. There I stood, with one

shoppers of all ages

shoe on. I watched the other shoe flop around as people passed

by it. **One little girl tugged at her mother's arm and said, "Look at that!" One**

man almost tripped over it and looked back with a frown. Then he smiled.

A crowd gathered around me, and many people offered

"Call the security guards," a man suggested. "They'll stop the escalator."

advice. Finally, a girl my age knocked the sandal loose.

("I'd hate to do that," I responded.)

Everyone cheered. ~~It was embarrassing.~~

I put on my sandal and tried to slink away without attracting any
more attention. I knew, though, that many shoppers would be
telling their families a funny story that evening.

Level 8   Unit 2   Personal Narrative   (Use with pupil book pages 77–78.)
Skill: Students will revise a story, improving the beginning and the ending, crossing out dull parts, and adding details and dialogue.

Name _____

THE WRITING PROCESS: PERSONAL NARRATIVE

RETEACHING WORKBOOK 16

Step 4: Proofread

When you proofread, look for mistakes in spelling, capitalization, and punctuation. Use proofreading marks to make corrections.

the beginning of september is always busy, said Ed.

Proofreading Marks

Symbol	Meaning	Symbol	Meaning	Symbol	Meaning
¶	Indent.	⋀	Add a comma.	≡	Capitalize.
⋀	Add something.	∼	Reverse the order.	/	Make a small letter.
⊙	Add a period.	ℐ	Take out.	∨∨	Add quotation marks.

Proofread the following story. There are three spelling mistakes, two run-on sentences, two sentence fragments, four punctuation errors, and four capitalization errors. Correct the errors. Use a dictionary to check your spelling.

In the middle of the night, Leo let out a realy loud yell. "It's a bear!" he

shouted.   "I can see its eyes shining in the bushes."

Everyone came running from the tents. We all talked at once.   "You must have

imagined it, Leo."

Leo pointed his flashlight. Toward the bushes.

"Don't do that, or the Bear will come here," Stu said.

"I thought you didn't believe me," Leo grimned.

We all looked at each other. Nobody said anything.   Just in case, we silently

grabed our sleeping bags and moved. Into the log Cabin.

The next morning we found a big raccoon that was sound asleep right outside

the tents. "Is this your bear?" we asked Leo.

Level 8   Unit 2   Personal Narrative   (Use with pupil book pages 79–80.)
Skill: Students will proofread a story, correcting mistakes in spelling, punctuation, and capitalization.

T8

Name _____

RETEACHING WORKBOOK 17

LANGUAGE AND USAGE

1 | Kinds of Nouns

▶ A common noun names any person, place, thing, or idea.
▶ A proper noun names a particular person, place, thing, or idea.
▶ A concrete noun names something that can be touched or seen.
▶ An abstract noun names an idea, a feeling, or a quality.

Common: doctor   zoo   river   document
Proper: Doctor Klea   Bronx Zoo   Hudson River   Bill of Rights
Concrete: library   Ohio River   Italians   referee   motorboats
Abstract: lateness   Arbor Day   liberty   publicity   puzzlement

Write each noun. Label it *common* or *proper* and then *concrete* or *abstract*.

Example: The students were studying history.
students—common, concrete   history—common, abstract

1. A huge fire once nearly destroyed Chicago.
   fire—common, concrete   Chicago—proper, concrete

2. The blaze lit up the sky like the Fourth of July.
   blaze—common, concrete   sky—common, concrete
   Fourth of July—proper, abstract

3. The flames had a major effect on the future of this city.
   flames—common, concrete   effect—common, abstract
   future—common, abstract   city—common, concrete

4. The cause of this event has become a legend.
   cause—common, abstract   event—common, abstract
   legend—common, abstract

5. In a barn owned by the O'Learys, a cow kicked over a lantern.
   barn—common, concrete   O'Learys—proper, concrete
   cow—common, concrete   lantern—common, concrete

6. Oddly enough, the O'Learys' cottage did not burn to the ground.
   cottage—common, concrete   ground—common, concrete

Level 8 Unit 3 Nouns   *(Use with pupil book pages 88–89.)*
Skill: Students will identify common, proper, concrete, and abstract nouns.

Name _____

RETEACHING WORKBOOK 18

LANGUAGE AND USAGE

2 | Compound and Collective Nouns

▶ A compound noun is made up of two or more words.
▶ A collective noun names a group of people, animals, or things.

Compound Nouns: spaceport   self-control   space probe   Martin Luther King
Collective Nouns: class   committee   flock   community

A. Write the compound noun in each sentence.

Example: A crowd gathered near the launch pad.   launch pad

1. Reaching outer space had always been one of our greatest dreams.   outer space

2. On July 20, 1969, the *Eagle*, a small spacecraft, landed on the moon.   spacecraft

3. Neil Armstrong became the first human to set foot upon the moon's surface.   Neil Armstrong

4. Edwin E. Aldrin, Jr., his copilot, joined him.   Edwin E. Aldrin, Jr.

5. The astronauts brought back close-ups of the moon's surface.   close-ups

6. From liftoff to landing, it was a historic flight.   liftoff

B. Write the collective noun in each sentence.

Example: A crowd of people applauded enthusiastically.   crowd

7. Everyone watched the members of the space crew appear.   crew

8. A scout troop waved a "Welcome Home" banner.   troop

9. A school band played the national anthem.   band

10. The public celebrated our country's first moon landing.   public

11. Our class watched on television.   class

12. All over the nation, many groups watched this event.   groups

Level 8 Unit 3 Nouns   *(Use with pupil book pages 90–91.)*
Skill: Students will identify compound and collective nouns.

Name _____

LANGUAGE AND USAGE | RETEACHING WORKBOOK

3 Singular and Plural Nouns

▶ To form the plural of most singular nouns, add s.
▶ To form the plural of nouns ending with s, x, z, sh, or ch, add es.
▶ Some nouns have special plural forms.

Singular Nouns: ant bunch belief sky   life   woman dues series
Plural Nouns: ants bunches beliefs skies lives women dues series

Singular Nouns: crisis son-in-law   close-up Macy   6 and
Plural Nouns: crises sons-in-law close-ups Macys 6's and's

Write the plural form of each noun. Use your dictionary if necessary.

Example: get-together — **get-togethers**

1. sandwich — **sandwiches**
2. McCoy — **McCoys**
3. radio — **radios**
4. turkey — **turkeys**
5. buzz — **buzzes**
6. mouse — **mice**
7. tongs — **tongs**
8. & — **&'s**
9. great-uncle — **great-uncles**
10. editor in chief — **editors in chief**
11. beach — **beaches**
12. guess — **guesses**
13. physics — **physics**
14. scissors — **scissors**
15. squeeze play — **squeeze plays**
16. sister-in-law — **sisters-in-law**
17. life — **lives**
18. piano — **pianos**
19. spoonful — **spoonfuls**
20. deer — **deer**
21. goose — **geese**
22. alumnus — **alumni**
23. cuff — **cuffs**
24. family — **families**
25. potato — **potatoes**
26. box — **boxes**
27. child — **children**
28. dash — **dashes**
29. *but* — **but's**
30. onion — **onions**

Level 8 Unit 3 Nouns (Use with pupil book pages 92–94.)
Skill: Students will form plural nouns.

Name _____

LANGUAGE AND USAGE | RETEACHING WORKBOOK

4 Possessive Nouns

▶ A possessive noun shows ownership.
▶ To form the possessive of a singular noun, a plural noun not ending with s, or a compound noun, add an apostrophe and s.
▶ To form the possessive of a plural noun ending with s, add an apostrophe only.

Singular Possessive Nouns
my **nephew's** birthday
the **head of state's** office
Andrew Cass's wedding
Eve's and **Keisha's** houses

Plural Possessive Nouns
our **ponies'** stable
daughters-in-law's relatives
the **children's** teacher
Eve and Keisha's house

Write the correct possessive nouns to complete these phrases.

Example: the coats of the guests — the **guests'** coats

1. the office of the lawyers — the **lawyers'** office
2. the jobs that my sisters-in-law have — my **sisters-in-law's** jobs
3. the jeep belonging to the driver — the **driver's** jeep
4. money that Dan and Jay each have — **Dan's** and **Jay's** money
5. the suit worn by Tess — **Tess's** suit
6. the pens that the editors in chief own — the **editors in chief's** pens
7. the hat that belongs to the sheriff — the **sheriff's** hat
8. the food that the grandmothers made — the **grandmothers'** food
9. a dog that my aunt and uncle both own — my **aunt** and **uncle's** dog
10. the feathers of the turkeys — the **turkeys'** feathers
11. the antlers these deer have — these **deer's** antlers
12. the picture belonging to the Scotts — the **Scotts'** picture
13. the computer owned by John Celi — **John Celi's** computer
14. the movie the actress made — the **actress's** movie
15. a cat that Lee and Art own together — **Lee** and **Art's** cat

Level 8 Unit 3 Nouns (Use with pupil book pages 95–96.)
Skill: Students will form singular and plural possessive nouns.

Name _____

LANGUAGE AND USAGE

RETEACHING WORKBOOK 21

5 | Combining Sentences: Appositives

▶ An **appositive** is a noun or a phrase that identifies another noun.
▶ Use commas to set off an appositive that is not needed to complete the meaning of a sentence.

St. Augustine is on the coast of Florida.
St. Augustine is the oldest city in the nation.
                                appositive
St. Augustine, **the oldest city in the nation,** is on the coast of Florida.

Combine each pair of sentences by changing the underlined words into an appositive. Use commas where they are needed.

Example: St. Augustine attracts many tourists. It is a historical city in Florida.
          St. Augustine, a historical city in Florida, attracts many tourists.

1. The earliest settlement in the United States was founded in 1565.
   The settlement in the United States was St. Augustine.
   The earliest settlement in the United States, St. Augustine, was founded in 1565.

2. The city's central fortress was built by the Spanish people in the 1600s. The fortress was Castillo de San Marcos.
   The city's central fortress, Castillo de San Marcos, was built by the Spanish people in the 1600s.

3. It overlooks Matanzas Bay. The bay is the entrance to St. Augustine.
   It overlooks Matanzas Bay, the entrance to St. Augustine.

4. The fort's main purpose made this an ideal location.
   The purpose was the protection of Spanish ships.
   The fort's main purpose, the protection of Spanish ships, made this an ideal location.

5. The British explorer tried to capture St. Augustine.
   The British explorer was Sir Francis Drake.
   The British explorer Sir Francis Drake tried to capture St. Augustine.

6. The battles over the city ended when the United States bought Florida from Spain. The city was a strategic spot.
   The battles over the city, a strategic spot, ended when the United States bought Florida from Spain.

Level 8 Unit 3 Nouns   *(Use with pupil book pages 97–99.)*
Skill: Students will combine sentences, using appositives.

T11

Name _____

COMPOSITION SKILL: COMPARISON AND CONTRAST

RETEACHING WORKBOOK 23

Main Idea and Supporting Details

A **paragraph** is a group of sentences that has one main idea. All the sentences in the paragraph must support the main idea.

Read each of the following paragraphs. Write the main idea of each one. Draw a line through any sentence that does not support the main idea.

A. When I received a Great Dane puppy as a birthday present, I got a big surprise. I had always wanted a nice little pet, but Topaz was growing by the minute. Topaz was not only large, but she was strong as well. Usually I end up being dragged on one of our walks. ~~Topaz came from a litter of eight puppies.~~

   Main Idea: **When I received a Great Dane puppy as a birthday present, I got a big surprise.**

B. Now that I have Topaz, I have realized how many responsibilities there are in owning a dog. Dogs need shots, regular exercise, and attention. You have to teach dogs how to heel, come when called, and sit upon command. ~~I do not like walking Topaz in the rain.~~ ~~Topaz's funny habits keep the whole family laughing.~~

   Main Idea: **Now that I have Topaz, I have realized how many responsibilities there are in owning a dog.**

C. Many people agree that the North American spoon weevil is one of the least harmful insects. Their conclusion is based on several facts. In the first place, the spoon weevil never destroys crops or property. Secondly, it never stings or bites people or animals. Finally, it never makes too much noise. ~~The insects are named after their favorite recreational facility—the spoon.~~

   Main Idea: **Many people agree that the North American spoon weevil is one of the least harmful insects.**

Level 8 Unit 4 Comparison and Contrast   *(Use with pupil book pages 127–128.)*
Skill: Students will identify the main ideas in paragraphs and will identify sentences that do not support the main ideas.

COMPOSITION SKILL: COMPARISON AND CONTRAST

Topic Sentences

The **topic sentence** states the main idea of the paragraph. A good topic sentence states the main idea clearly and uses lively, exact language.

Each of the following paragraphs needs a better topic sentence. Read each paragraph and decide what the main idea is. Then write two good topic sentences to replace the underlined one. Put a check next to the topic sentence you like better.

Sample answers:

A.   I have seen some animals in the mountains. Early in the morning, while the sky is still gray, birds sing outside the windows of our cabin on the mountain. During the morning jays and sparrows flit in the sun. Yellow butterflies land on the flowers and tree branches. In the afternoon chipmunks scurry through the bushes. Rabbits dart across the clearing. At night raccoons scavenge for food from our garbage pails.

Topic Sentence: From morning until night, our cabin in the mountains is surrounded by the sights and sounds of nature.

Topic Sentence: From my cabin window, I can be an amateur biologist.

B.   Gilbert Stuart was an artist of the 1700s. George Washington was one of his famous subjects. Stuart painted three different portraits of George Washington between 1795 and 1796. Of the three portraits, none is more familiar than the one that appears on the dollar bill. Almost everyone knows whose face is on the bill, but few people know the identity of the artist who painted it.

Topic Sentence: Most people in the United States have seen Gilbert Stuart's art.

Topic Sentence: George Washington and the artist Gilbert Stuart made a terrific team.

COMPOSITION SKILL: COMPARISON AND CONTRAST

Organizing Comparison and Contrast Paragraphs

When you **compare** two things, explain how they are alike. When you **contrast** two things, explain how they are different.

Read the following pairs of topics for comparison and contrast paragraphs. Then choose one pair and follow the directions below.

field hockey and ice hockey	city living and country living
movies and stage plays	travel by car and by train

A. List two ways in which the two items you chose are alike. Then write a topic sentence that you could use for a paragraph comparing the two items.

Sample answers:

Similarities:

1.   Field hockey and ice hockey are both sports.

2.   Both sports use hockey sticks.

Topic Sentence for Comparison Paragraph: Playing field hockey and ice hockey requires similar skills.

B. Now list two differences between the two items in your topic. Then write a topic sentence that you could use for a paragraph contrasting the two items.

Sample answers:

Differences:

1.   Field hockey is played on a field, and ice hockey is played on ice.

2.   You wear sports sneakers to play field hockey and ice skates to play ice hockey.

Topic Sentence for Contrast Paragraph: Field hockey can be played anywhere that there is grass, but ice hockey is usually played at an ice rink.

Name _____

THE WRITING PROCESS: COMPARISON AND CONTRAST

Step 3: Revise

Have I	yes
included a topic sentence that states the main idea clearly?	☐
crossed out any sentences that do not belong?	☐
added examples and details to make the comparison clearer?	☐
replaced vague, fuzzy language with more exact words to make the meaning clear?	☐

Revise the following paragraph of comparison. Use the check list above to help you. Check off each box when you have finished your revision.
- Use a thesaurus to help find exact words.
- Use the space above each line, on the sides, and below the paragraph for your changes.

Sample answers:

My two best friends have a lot in common with each other. Both of my friends like movies, for instance. ~~Natalie likes~~

~~comedies, though, while Becky likes adventure stories.~~ Becky **to play softball and volleyball.** **any** likes ~~outdoor games.~~ Becky and I spend hours talking about ~~the~~ **problems we may have** **too** ~~stuff that is bothering us.~~ Natalie and I can talk for hours. Becky **and Natalie** **have good advice** **possible** almost always ~~has something helpful to say about~~ how ~~maybe I~~ **solutions for problems.** ~~could go about solving a problem. So does Natalie.~~ Becky is

~~really friendly and outgoing. Natalie tends to be quieter~~ and have **and interested in other people.** ~~just a few friends.~~ They're both really likable, ~~though.~~ I'm glad

they're my friends!

Natalie is good at horseback riding.

Name _____

THE WRITING PROCESS: COMPARISON AND CONTRAST

Step 4: Proofread

When you proofread, look for mistakes in spelling, punctuation, and capitalization. Use proofreading marks to correct the mistakes.

hobbies
One sister Elizabeth has many ~~hobby~~.

Proofreading Marks				
¶ Indent.	∧ Add a comma.	⊙ Add a period.	≡ Capitalize.	Add quotation marks.
∧ Add something.	∼ Reverse the order.	⟍ Take out.	/ Make a small letter.	

A. Proofread the following paragraph. There are two missing punctuation marks and two mistakes in capitalization. There are two spelling mistakes and one run-on sentence. Find these mistakes and correct them. Use a dictionary to check your spelling.

Two types of reptiles, alligators and crocodiles, have many things in common.

Both are large animals that live in rivers and swamps in tropical areas. The female

babies
Alligator lays its eggs near the water. It guards its nest and its ~~babys~~ carefully.

No one
similarly, the female Crocodile's nest is also along the shoreline. ~~Noone~~ should try

to get near either animal's nest.

B. Proofread the following paragraph. There is one run-on sentence, one capitalization error, two spelling errors, and two incorrect possessive nouns. Find and correct the errors.

In some ways, however, Alligators and crocodiles are very different in their

activities
appearance and ~~activitys~~. The crocodiles head is narrow and pointed the alligators

h
head, on the ~~oter~~ hand, is broad and rounded. Alligators are very noisy animals,

but crocodiles tend to be quieter.

UNIT 5 TEACHER'S ANNOTATED PAGES

Name _____

LANGUAGE AND USAGE   RETEACHING
                                      WORKBOOK **29**

1 Kinds of Verbs

▲ A **verb** expresses physical action, mental action, or being.
▲ A **linking verb** expresses being. It links the subject with a word in the
predicate that describes or identifies the subject.

Action Verbs: Farmers **use** natural resources.
They **grow** much of the world's food.
They **want** successful harvests.

Being Verbs: There **are** many different types of farms.
Farming **remains** an important occupation. *(linking verb)*
Farmers **grow** very strong from their work. *(linking verb)*

A. Write each underlined verb. Label it *action* or *being.*

Example: That farm on the hillside looks beautiful.   looks—being

1. We visited a farm last week.   visited—action
2. A friend of mine works there.   works—action
3. Work on a farm seems difficult.   seems—being
4. There are different chores for every season.   are—being
5. Farmers rise early in the morning.   rise—action
6. Their schedule sounds exhausting.   sounds—being
7. For many farmers the hard work is worthwhile.   is—being
8. They enjoy their independence.   enjoy—action

B. Write each underlined verb. Label it *action* or *linking.*

Example: We tasted the newly picked beans.   tasted—action

9. Farmers grow accustomed to weather changes.   grow—linking
10. At times storms appear without warning.   appear—action
11. Farmers look for signs of weather patterns.   look—action
12. Their crops grow best in certain conditions.   grow—action
13. Plants look healthier after a good season.   look—linking
14. They taste better as well.   taste—linking

Level 8 Unit 5 Verbs   *(Use with pupil book pages 146–147.)*
Skill: Students will identify action and linking verbs.

Name _____

LANGUAGE AND USAGE   RETEACHING
                                      WORKBOOK **30**

2 Verb Phrases

▲ A **verb phrase** includes a main verb and one or more helping verbs.
▲ The **main verb** expresses the action or being.
▲ The **helping verb** or verbs help complete the meaning of the main verb.

Helping Verbs   Main Verbs
William Penn **had   proposed** plans for Philadelphia in 1682.
I'm   visiting the city today.
We **didn't   see** the Liberty Bell on our last trip.
Have you ever **been** to Philadelphia?

Write the verb phrase in each sentence.

Example: Philadelphia is located on the Delaware River. _____ **is located**

1. Do you remember William Penn from your study of American history?
   Do remember

2. Penn had always dreamed of a "city of brotherly love."
   had dreamed

3. Philadelphia could have been the nation's capital.
   could have been

4. Philadelphia did become an important city in colonial America.
   did become

5. Would you have enjoyed Philadelphia in the 1600s?
   Would have enjoyed

6. I just can't imagine it during the seventeenth century.
   can imagine

7. Benjamin Franklin was living in Philadelphia in 1723.
   was living

8. He'd been looking for work in the large city.
   had been looking

Level 8 Unit 5 Verbs   *(Use with pupil book pages 148–149.)*
Skill: Students will identify verb phrases.

T14

Name _____

LANGUAGE AND USAGE

3 Tenses

> ► Every verb has four **principal parts**.
> ► Verbs have different **tenses** to express different times.
> ► Use the principal parts of a verb to form its tenses.

Verb	Present Participle	Past	Past Participle
walk	(is) walking	walked	(has) walked

Present Tense: I **carry** the flag.
Past Tense: I **carried** the flag.
Future Tense: I **will carry** the flag.
Present Perfect Tense: We **have stopped** for a rest.
Past Perfect Tense: We **had stopped** for a rest.
Future Perfect Tense: We **will have stopped** for a rest.

A. Write the three simple tense forms of each verb with *they*.

Example: work they ___work___, they ___worked___ they ___will work___

1. open they **open** they **opened** they **will open**

2. drop they **drop** they **dropped** they **will drop**

3. close they **close** they **closed** they **will close**

4. marry they **marry** they **married** they **will marry**

B. Write each sentence, using the tense of the verb shown in parentheses.

Example: The city __?__ upon a plan for the park. **(decide—present perfect)**

    The city has decided upon a plan for the park.

5. The concrete in the old pool __?__ . **(crack—past perfect)**
The concrete in the old pool had cracked.

6. Workers __?__ it by next summer. **(fix—future perfect)**
Workers will have fixed it by next summer.

7. A local store __?__ paint for the weathered picnic tables. **(supply—past)**
A local store supplied paint for the weathered picnic tables.

8. Volunteers __?__ a day for the litter pickup. **(plan—present perfect)**
Volunteers have planned a day for the litter pickup.

Name _____

LANGUAGE AND USAGE

4 Forms of *be, have,* and *do*

> ► You can use *be, have,* and *do* as main verbs and as helping verbs.
> ► *Be, have,* and *do* have different forms for different subjects and for different tenses.

Subjects	Forms of *be*	Forms of *have*	Forms of *do*
I	am, was	have, had	do, did
he, she, it	is, was	has, had	does, did
singular nouns	is, was	has, had	does, did
we, you, they	are, were	have, had	do, did
plural nouns	are, were	have, had	do, did

Write the correct form of the verb in parentheses to complete each sentence.

Example: A zoo ___is___ a place with many animals. **(is, are)**

1. A large zoo **has** animals from all over the world. **(has, have)**

2. Most zoo animals **are** in cages. **(is, are)**

3. **Don't** some animals live in open areas? **(Doesn't, Don't)**

4. Why **do** people visit zoos? **(does, do)**

5. We **are** fascinated by the way animals look and behave. **(is, are)**

6. Zoos **don't** only provide entertainment. **(doesn't, don't)**

7. They **are** also laboratories for zoologists. **(is, are)**

8. What **does** a zoologist do? **(does, do)**

9. Zoology **is** the study of animals. **(is, are)**

10. The first known zoo **was** in Egypt in about 1500 B.C. **(was, were)**

11. An Egyptian queen **had** a collection of animals. **(have, had)**

12. **Does** it attract great interest? **(Does, Do)**

13. Many zoos **have** beautiful gardens. **(has, have)**

14. The word *zoo* **is** short for "zoological garden." **(is, are)**

15. **Were** you at the zoo last week? **(Was, Were)**

16. I **am** visiting our zoo on Tuesday. **(am, are)**

UNIT 5 TEACHER'S ANNOTATED PAGES

Name _____

LANGUAGE AND USAGE   RETEACHING WORKBOOK **34**

6 | More Irregular Verbs

▶ You must learn the principal parts of irregular verbs.

Verb	Present Participle	Past	Past Participle
begin	(is) beginning	began	(has) begun
ring	(is) ringing	rang	(has) rung
choose	(is) choosing	chose	(has) chosen
see	(is) seeing	saw	(has) seen

Write the missing principal parts of the following irregular verbs.

	Present Participle	Past	Past Participle
Example: sink	(is) sinking	sank	(has) sunk
1. break	**(is) breaking**	**broke**	**(has) broken**
2. drive	**(is) driving**	**drove**	**(has) driven**
3. speak	**(is) speaking**	**spoke**	**(has) spoken**
4. wear	**(is) wearing**	**wore**	**(has) worn**
5. give	**(is) giving**	**gave**	**(has) given**
6. forget	**(is) forgetting**	**forgot**	**(has) forgotten**
7. drink	**(is) drinking**	**drank**	**(has) drunk**
8. lie	**(is) lying**	**lay**	**(has) laid**
9. swim	**(is) swimming**	**swam**	**(has) swum**
10. grow	**(is) growing**	**grew**	**(has) grown**
11. sing	**(is) singing**	**sang**	**(has) sung**
12. freeze	**(is) freezing**	**froze**	**(has) frozen**
13. write	**(is) writing**	**wrote**	**(has) written**
14. eat	**(is) eating**	**ate**	**(has) eaten**

Level 8 Unit 5 Verbs   *(Use with pupil book pages 158–159.)*
Skill: Students will form the principal parts of irregular verbs.

Name _____

LANGUAGE AND USAGE   RETEACHING WORKBOOK **33**

5 | Irregular Verbs

▶ **Irregular verbs** do not follow any rules for forming the past and the past participle. You must learn the principal parts of irregular verbs.

Verb	Present Participle	Past	Past Participle
be	(is) being	was, were	(has) been
have	(is) having	had	(has) had
do	(is) doing	did	(has) done
put	(is) putting	put	(has) put
run	(is) running	ran	(has) run
bring	(is) bringing	brought	(has) brought
make	(is) making	made	(has) made

A. Write the missing principal parts of the following irregular verbs.

	Present Participle	Past	Past Participle
Example: have	(is) having	had	(has) had
1. hold	**(is) holding**	**held**	**(has) held**
2. hurt	**(is) hurting**	**hurt**	**(has) hurt**
3. find	**(is) finding**	**found**	**(has) found**
4. leave	**(is) leaving**	**left**	**(has) left**
5. win	**(is) winning**	**won**	**(has) won**
6. let	**(is) letting**	**let**	**(has) let**
7. read	**(is) reading**	**read**	**(has) read**
8. burst	**(is) bursting**	**burst**	**(has) burst**
9. set	**(is) setting**	**set**	**(has) set**
10. catch	**(is) catching**	**caught**	**(has) caught**
11. cost	**(is) costing**	**cost**	**(has) cost**
12. come	**(is) coming**	**came**	**(has) come**
13. think	**(is) thinking**	**thought**	**(has) thought**

Level 8 Unit 5 Verbs   *(Use with pupil book pages 155–157.)*
Skill: Students will form the principal parts of irregular verbs.

T16

Name _____

RETEACHING WORKBOOK 35

LANGUAGE AND USAGE

7 | Progressive Forms

- Each tense has a **progressive form** to express continuing action.
- Form the progressive with an appropriate tense of *be* plus the present participle.

Present Progressive: The students **are rehearsing**.
Past Progressive: They **were rehearsing** yesterday.
Future Progressive: They **will be rehearsing** tomorrow.
Present Perfect Progressive: They **have been rehearsing** all day.
Past Perfect Progressive: They **had been rehearsing** earlier.
Future Perfect Progressive: They **will have been rehearsing** for three hours by the end of the day.

Write the progressive verb form in each sentence.

Example: The director was taking attendance. **was taking**

1. The eighth grade students are preparing for a play next week. **are preparing**
2. They will be presenting *My Fair Lady*. **will be presenting**
3. The music teacher has been working very hard with the actors. **has been working**
4. The director had been holding rehearsals three days a week. **had been holding**
5. The cast is meeting every day after school. **is meeting**
6. The students were practicing their lines yesterday. **were practicing**
7. They will have been rehearsing for six weeks by the time of the performance. **will have been rehearsing**
8. They have been selling many tickets. **have been selling**
9. A large crowd will be attending the play. **will be attending**
10. Everyone is hoping for a big hit. **is hoping**

Level 8 Unit 5 Verbs *(Use with pupil book pages 160–161.)*
Skill: Students will identify progressive verb forms.

Name _____

RETEACHING WORKBOOK 36

LANGUAGE AND USAGE

8 | Transitive and Intransitive Verbs

- A **transitive verb** expresses action that is directed toward a word in the predicate.
- The word to which the action is directed is the **object of the verb**.
- An **intransitive verb** does not have an object.
- Linking verbs are always intransitive.

Transitive Verbs   **Intransitive Verbs**
Viking explorers **named** Greenland.   Greenland **lies** in the North Atlantic.
New lands **attracted** them.   Greenland **is** an island.

Write each underlined verb. Label it *transitive* or *intransitive*.

Example: Sarah <u>displayed</u> a map of Greenland.   **displayed—transitive**

1. Greenland <u>is</u> the largest island in the world.   **is—intransitive**
2. An ice cap almost <u>covers</u> the island.   **covers—transitive**
3. Fifty-four thousand people <u>live</u> in Greenland.   **live—intransitive**
4. Many islanders <u>fish</u> for a living.   **fish—intransitive**
5. Greenland <u>has</u> some farms.   **has—transitive**
6. The farmers <u>grow</u> various crops.   **grow—transitive**
7. Some farmers on the island <u>raise</u> sheep.   **raise—transitive**
8. No forests <u>exist</u> in Greenland.   **exist—intransitive**
9. Very few tourists ever <u>visit</u> Greenland.   **visit—transitive**
10. Some people <u>see</u> the ice cap from an airplane.   **see—transitive**
11. The weather <u>stays</u> cold much of the year.   **stays—intransitive**
12. Some people <u>speak</u> Greenlandic.   **speak—transitive**
13. Danish <u>is</u> also an official language.   **is—intransitive**
14. Most of Greenland <u>lies</u> within the Arctic Circle.   **lies—intransitive**
15. Dog sleds <u>carry</u> Greenlanders over the snow.   **carry—transitive**

Level 8 Unit 5 Verbs *(Use with pupil book pages 162–163.)*
Skill: Students will identify transitive and intransitive verbs.

T17

UNIT 5 TEACHER'S ANNOTATED PAGES

Name _____

LANGUAGE AND USAGE   RETEACHING WORKBOOK

9 Direct and Indirect Objects

- The **direct object** tells *who* or *what* receives the action of a transitive verb.
- The **indirect object** is a noun or a pronoun in the predicate that tells *to whom*, *for whom*, or *for what* the action is done.

                        direct   direct
Robots do many **jobs** and **chores**. They do **them** well.
      indirect   direct   indirect direct
Scientists give **robots commands**. They give **them orders** quickly.

Write each object. Then label it *direct* or *indirect*. The verbs are underlined to help you.

Example: Albert gave the robot a name.
           robot—**indirect**, name—**direct**

1. Many factories use special robots. **robots—direct**

2. Engineers assign them tasks on assembly lines.
   them—indirect, tasks—direct

3. Robots can give cars a perfect paint job.
   cars—indirect, job—direct

4. In households robots save people time and trouble.
   people—indirect, time—direct, trouble—direct

5. Some robots wash dishes and floors. **dishes—direct, floors—direct**

6. They will do these things and other tasks with no complaint.
   things—direct, tasks—direct

7. Robots occasionally disappoint their creators and owners.
   creators—direct, owners—direct

8. The manufacturer sold Albert and me a defective robot.
   Albert—indirect, me—indirect, robot—direct

Level 8 Unit 5 Verbs   (Use with pupil book pages 164–166.)
Skill: Students will identify direct and indirect objects.

Name _____

LANGUAGE AND USAGE   RETEACHING WORKBOOK

10 Predicate Nouns and Predicate Adjectives

- Predicate nouns and predicate adjectives follow linking verbs.
- A **predicate noun** identifies or renames the subject.
- A **predicate adjective** describes the subject.

Predicate Nouns: Keith is a hard **worker** and a good **friend**.
Predicate Adjective: He looks **kind**.

Write the underlined words. Label them *predicate noun* or *predicate adjective*.

Example: The small radios are convenient.
           convenient—**predicate adjective**

1. Radios have been common items for many years.
   items—predicate noun

2. Today stereo headsets seem almost equally popular.
   popular—predicate adjective

3. Headsets have grown increasingly lightweight and sophisticated.
   lightweight, sophisticated—predicate adjectives

4. The items appeared harmless at first.
   harmless—predicate adjective

5. They were simply modern conveniences.
   conveniences—predicate noun

6. Recently, however, headsets have become a matter for concern.
   matter—predicate noun

7. Two possible hazards are accidents and ear damage.
   accidents, damage—predicate nouns

8. Many health officials remain doubtful about the safety of headsets.
   doubtful—predicate adjective

Level 8 Unit 5 Verbs   (Use with pupil book pages 167–168.)
Skill: Students will identify predicate nouns and predicate adjectives.

T18

Name _____

LANGUAGE AND USAGE

RETEACHING
WORKBOOK
39

11 | Active and Passive Voices

▶ A verb is in the **active voice** if the subject performs the action.
▶ A verb is in the **passive voice** if the subject receives the action.
▶ Use the passive voice when the doer of an action is unimportant.
▶ Use the active voice for direct, forceful sentences.

                      verb   direct object

Active Voice: The dogs **found** the hikers.

                 subject   verb

Passive Voice: The hikers **were found** by the dogs.

Underline the verb in each sentence. Then label the verb *active* or *passive*.

Example: Some dogs <u>search</u> for missing persons.   active

1. Rescue dogs are <u>trained</u> by special workers.   passive

2. The animals <u>locate</u> lost individuals.   active

3. The dogs are <u>given</u> a scent from clothing.   passive

4. The clothing <u>belongs</u> to the missing person.   active

5. Then the dogs <u>follow</u> the smell.   active

6. Police <u>use</u> bloodhounds as search dogs.   active

7. Criminals are <u>found</u> by the animals.   passive

8. Bloodhounds are <u>used</u> often in night searches.   passive

9. They <u>have</u> very poor eyesight.   active

10. Therefore, bloodhounds <u>rely</u> on their sense of smell.   active

11. Sometimes a scent can be <u>masked</u> by other odors.   passive

12. A scent is <u>weakened</u> by water or dampness.   passive

13. The dogs usually <u>prove</u> their value though.   active

14. Some dogs have <u>tracked</u> people across rivers.   active

15. Others have <u>discovered</u> people under snow.   active

16. One person was <u>found</u> under fourteen feet of snow.   passive

Level 8 Unit 5 Verbs   *(Use with pupil book pages 169–170.)*
Skill: Students will identify active and passive verbs.

Name _____

LANGUAGE AND USAGE

RETEACHING
WORKBOOK
40

12 | Subject-Verb Agreement

▶ A subject and its verb must agree in number.
▶ Use a plural verb with a compound subject joined by *and*.
▶ Use a verb that agrees with the nearer of two subjects joined by *or* or *nor*.

Singular Subjects: The geologist **studies** fossils.
                            He **learns** about the past.

Plural Subjects: Fossils **provide** clues about living things.
                            They **require** careful study.

Compound Subjects: Teachers and students **learn** from fossils.
                               Either geologists or a student **collects** the fossils.
                               Neither the technique nor the tools **are** perfect.

Write the verb in parentheses that agrees with the underlined subject.

Example: <u>Scientists</u> (collects, collect) fossils.   collect

1. A <u>fossil</u> (contain, contains) animal or plant remains.   contains

2. <u>Fossils</u> (is, are) studied in many ways.   are

3. The scientist and her <u>assistant</u> (handle, handles) fossils carefully.   handle

4. Either the scientist or her <u>assistants</u> (cleans, clean) the fossil.   clean

5. Either chemicals or plain <u>soap</u> (is, are) used for cleaning.   is

6. Small hand tools and power <u>tools</u> also (helps, help).   help

7. The <u>scientist</u> (wants, want) to know the age of a fossil.   wants

8. <u>She</u> (uses, use) an x-ray and radioactive dating methods.   uses

9. Neither the x-ray nor radioactive dating <u>methods</u> (tells, tell) the exact age of the fossil.   tell

10. Instead <u>they</u> (provides, provide) approximate ages.   provide

11. <u>Scientists</u> (learns, learn) a lot from this information.   learn

12. <u>It</u> (tells, tell) about the history of the earth.   tells

13. Neither the earth's <u>landforms</u> nor its wildlife (has, have) remained the same.   has

14. A plant trace or animal <u>fossils</u> (records, record) the changes.   record

Level 8 Unit 5 Verbs   *(Use with pupil book pages 171–172.)*
Skill: Students will choose verbs to agree with singular, plural, and compound subjects.

T19

Name _____

LANGUAGE AND USAGE   RETEACHING WORKBOOK **41**

13 ‖ More About Subject-Verb Agreement

▶ Use a singular verb with a title or a name of a single thing, with a collective noun referring to a whole group, and with a noun of amount.
▶ Use a plural verb with a collective noun referring to the individual members of a group and with a noun of amount when referring to the individual units.

    Titles: *Hard Times* **is** a book by Charles Dickens.
    Names: Max and Weber **is** my favorite clothing store.
    Nouns Ending with s: Mathematics **is** challenging.
         The scissors **are** in the sewing box.
    Collective Nouns: The audience **claps** loudly.
         The audience **react** in different ways.
    Nouns of Amounts: Ten dollars **is** a lot of money.
         The ten dollars **were** set side by side.

Write the verb in parentheses that agrees with the underlined subject.

Example: The eighth grade <u>class</u> (is, are) having a party.   **is**

1. Three <u>weeks</u> (is, are) enough time to plan a party.   **is**
2. <u>News</u> of the party (has, have) traveled fast.   **has**
3. <u>Josie's Meatballs</u> (is, are) catering the dinner.   **is**
4. <u>Six dollars</u> (seem, seems) like a fair price for a ticket.   **seems**
5. The decoration <u>crew</u> (works, work) hard.   **works**
6. The <u>group</u> (is, are) all doing different jobs.   **are**
7. The art <u>club</u> (has, have) made a beautiful mural.   **has**
8. A string <u>quartet</u> (is, are) going to perform.   **is**
9. <u>Actors Unlimited</u> (is, are) performing a scene from a book.   **is**
10. <u>The Adventures of Tom Sawyer</u> (is, are) the book.   **is**
11. The planning <u>committee</u> (has, have) suggested a dress code.   **has**
12. <u>Denim pants</u> (do, does) not suit the occasion.   **do**
13. Only three <u>quarters</u> (is, are) now left in the treasury.   **are**
14. Perhaps <u>economics</u> (is, are) not the class's best subject.   **is**

Level 8   Unit 5   **Verbs**   *(Use with pupil book pages 173–175.)*
Skill: Students will choose verbs to agree with titles, names, collective nouns, nouns ending with s, and nouns of amount.

Name _____

LANGUAGE AND USAGE   RETEACHING WORKBOOK **42**

14 ‖ Agreement in Inverted and Interrupted Order

▶ The subject of a sentence in **inverted** or **interrupted order** follows all or part of the predicate.
▶ First, find the subject. Then make the verb agree with it.

    Inverted Order: On the news **are** maps of the weather.
         There **are** two maps on the wall.
         Have you ever **watched** the weather report?
    Interrupted Order: The meteorologists on television **report** the weather.
         Ms. Chu, one of the meteorologists, **predicts** the weather.

Write the verb in parentheses that agrees with each underlined subject.

Example: <u>Maps</u> on television (is, are) not true weather maps.   **are**

1. (Does, Do) most <u>people</u> understand a true weather map?   **Do**
2. Usually there (is, are) too much <u>information</u> for us.   **is**
3. On the news <u>programs</u> (is, are) simpler maps.   **are**
4. How (does, do) <u>you</u> forecast the weather?   **do**
5. <u>Changes</u> in the weather (gives, give) important clues.   **give**
6. The movement of air <u>masses</u> (tells, tell) meteorologists a lot.   **tells**
7. A "low," one of the air-pressure <u>centers</u>, (signals, signal) oncoming storms.   **signals**
8. Why (is, are) the <u>weather</u> so hard to predict?   **is**
9. There (is, are) so many <u>factors</u> to consider.   **are**
10. Mark Twain, one of our most famous <u>writers</u>, (sums, sum) it up well.   **sums**
11. What (is, are) his famous <u>remark</u> about weather?   **is**
12. In this book (is, are) the <u>quotation</u>.   **is**
13. The quotation, one of Twain's witty <u>sayings</u>, (says, say) "Everybody talks about the weather, but nobody does anything about it."   **says**
14. The control of weather <u>conditions</u> (remains, remain) beyond our abilities.   **remains**

Level 8   Unit 5   **Verbs**   *(Use with pupil book pages 176–177.)*
Skill: Students will choose verbs to agree with singular and plural subjects of sentences in inverted order and interrupted order.

UNIT 5   TEACHER'S ANNOTATED PAGES

T20

Name _____

RETEACHING WORKBOOK 44

LANGUAGE AND USAGE

16 | affect, effect; accept, except

- The verb *affect* means "to influence."
- The verb *effect* means "to cause to happen."
- The noun *effect* means "result."
- The verb *accept* means "to receive."
- The preposition *except* means "excluding."

> The new rules **will affect** everyone.
> The rules **should effect** many changes.
> Their **effect** will be felt quickly.
> The committee **accepted** most of the suggestions.
> The members agreed with all the ideas **except** one.

Rewrite each sentence, using the correct word in parentheses.

Example: The drought (affects, effects) three counties.
The drought affects three counties.

1. (Accept, Except) for last weekend, it has been a dry summer.
   Except for last weekend, it has been a dry summer.

2. The weather has had a serious (affect, effect) on the local crops.
   The weather has had a serious effect on the local crops.

3. The lack of rain has (affected, effected) the reservoirs as well.
   The lack of rain has affected the reservoirs as well.

4. The water commission must (affect, effect) changes in water use.
   The water commission must effect changes in water use.

5. Lin Lee has (accepted, excepted) a position on the Drought Emergency Team.
   Lin Lee has accepted a position on the Drought Emergency Team.

6. She has visited every town in the area (accept, except) Pine Bluff.
   She has visited every town in the area except Pine Bluff.

7. Most people are (accepting, excepting) the new water restrictions.
   Most people are accepting the new water restrictions.

8. The only way to (affect, effect) change is for everyone to cooperate.
   The only way to effect change is for everyone to cooperate.

Level 8 Unit 5 Verbs (Use with pupil book page 179.)
Skill: Students will use *affect, effect, accept,* and *except* correctly.

Name _____

RETEACHING WORKBOOK 43

LANGUAGE AND USAGE

15 | lie, lay; rise, raise

- Use *lie* for "to rest or to remain." *Lie* is intransitive.
- Use *lay* for "to put or to place." *Lay* is transitive.
- Use *rise* for "to get up." *Rise* is intransitive.
- Use *raise* for "to lift or to grow." *Raise* is transitive.

>   direct object
> Martha **will lie** down soon. She **will lay** her coat on the chair.
>   direct object
> She **will rise** after a short nap. She **will raise** the shades.

Rewrite each sentence, using the correct verb form in parentheses.

Example: Martha (raises, rises) vegetables in her garden.
Martha raises vegetables in her garden.

1. Martha (raised, rose) early this morning.
   Martha rose early this morning.

2. Everyone else in the family was still (lying, laying) in bed.
   Everyone else in the family was still lying in bed.

3. Martha had (lain, laid) her tools out the night before.
   Martha had laid her tools out the night before.

4. It is hard work to (raise, rise) vegetables.
   It is hard work to raise vegetables.

5. Martha (raises, rises) carrots and onions.
   Martha raises carrots and onions.

6. She carefully (lay, laid) the seeds in the soil.
   She carefully laid the seeds in the soil.

7. A quarter of an inch of soil (lay, laid) on top of them.
   A quarter of an inch of soil lay on top of them.

8. A few weeks later tiny seedlings (raised, rose) from the ground.
   A few weeks later tiny seedlings rose from the ground.

Level 8 Unit 5 Verbs (Use with pupil book page 178.)
Skill: Students will use *lie, lay, rise,* and *raise* correctly.

T21

Plot

> The **plot** of most stories follows this pattern: one or more characters have a problem, or **conflict**; the conflict builds to a **climax**; and the climax is followed by the **resolution**, or solution to the conflict.

Read the following plot summary. Then write one or two sentences, telling the conflict, the climax, and the resolution of the plot.

   In one part of Mark Twain's *The Adventures of Tom Sawyer*, Tom finds that he has to whitewash, or paint, a fence along the sidewalk. It is a long, hard job, and he would like to get out of it. When some of his friends come by, Tom begins to give them a ''sales talk'' about what an important and demanding job whitewashing a fence is. Eventually, Tom does not have to paint the fence at all, because his friends have convinced themselves that it is something they really want to do. Tom concludes that work is something you have to do, while play is something you don't have to do.

Sample answers:

Conflict: Tom Sawyer does not want to whitewash a fence along the sidewalk.

Climax: Tom ''sells'' the job of whitewashing the fence to some of his friends by making the job seem more important and difficult than it is.

Resolution: Tom does not have to paint the fence because his friends do it.

Level 8 Unit 6 Story   (Use with pupil book pages 214–215.)
Skill: Students will identify the conflict, climax, and resolution of a story plot.

T22

Setting

> The particular place and time of a story are the **setting**. When you describe a setting, choose words and details that bring out a particular **mood**, or feeling surrounding the events.

Four settings in which a story might take place are listed below. List four words or details that create a mood of loneliness, mysteriousness, happiness, or excitement for each setting.

A.   A small New England town

   1.   **Answers will vary.**

   2.   _____

   3.   _____

   4.   _____

B.   A camp in the Rocky Mountains

   1.   _____

   2.   _____

   3.   _____

   4.   _____

C.   A country fair

   1.   _____

   2.   _____

   3.   _____

   4.   _____

D.   A downtown street in a large city

   1.   _____

   2.   _____

   3.   _____

   4.   _____

Level 8 Unit 6 Story   (Use with pupil book pages 215–216.)
Skill: Students will write details for four story settings, creating moods of loneliness, mysteriousness, happiness, or excitement.

UNIT 6   TEACHER'S ANNOTATED PAGES

COMPOSITION SKILL: STORY

Characters

Any person or animal that takes part in the action of a story is a **character**. There are five main ways to show what a character is like. You can describe the character's personality and appearance. You can have the character speak or have another character speak about him or her. You can also show what the character does.

Imagine what each character below might be like. Then write one sentence to describe each character's appearance, personality or feelings, and actions.

A. A girl or boy six years of age

Appearance: *Answers will vary.* _____

_____

Personality or Feelings: _____

_____

Actions: _____

B. A grandmother who owns her own business

Appearance: _____

_____

Personality or Feelings: _____

_____

Actions: _____

C. A bus driver or train conductor

Appearance: _____

_____

Personality or Feelings: _____

_____

Actions: _____

Level 8 Unit 6 Story *(Use with pupil book pages 217–218.)*
Skill: Students will show what characters are like by describing their appearance, personality or feelings, and actions.

COMPOSITION SKILL: STORY

Point of View

When you write a story, choose a **point of view** from which to tell it. A **limited point of view** tells what one character in the story thinks, feels, and sees. The story can be told in the **first person** (*I*) or the **third person** (*he* or *she*).

An **omniscient**, or **all-knowing**, **point of view** tells what all the characters in a story think, feel, and see. A story with this point of view is usually told in the third person.

The following paragraph from a story is told from a limited point of view. Rewrite the story from the point of view of an all-knowing narrator who can tell what all the characters think, feel, and see. The first sentence is provided below.

I was looking around the classroom nervously as the teacher passed out the tests. She didn't look worried at all. In fact, she looked as if she was in a good mood. I could see Lydia staring at something on the windowsill, but I couldn't tell what. She seemed relaxed. Looking back, I saw Paul, who was tapping his pencil.

Omniscient Point of View:

Everyone in the classroom had different thoughts and feelings as the tests were being passed out. *Answers will vary.* _____

_____

_____

_____

_____

_____

_____

Level 8 Unit 6 Story *(Use with pupil book pages 219–221.)*
Skill: Students will rewrite a paragraph from a story, changing the point of view from limited to omniscient.

Name _____

THE WRITING PROCESS: STORY

RETEACHING WORKBOOK 50

Step 4: Proofread

When you proofread, look for mistakes in spelling, capitalization, punctuation, and grammar. Use proofreading marks to make corrections.

Tom asked for tomatos from /our garden⊙

Proofreading Marks

¶ Indent.	∧ Add a comma.	⊙ Add a period.	≡ Capitalize.
∧ Add something.	∿ Reverse the order.	ℐ Take out.	/ Make a small letter.
			∨∨ Add quotation marks.

A. Proofread the following paragraphs. There are two spelling errors, one capitalization error, one wrong punctuation mark, one mistake in paragraph format, and two verbs in the wrong tense. Correct the errors. Use a dictionary to check your spelling.

Bryan was excited about the race the next day. At dinner his sister tammy had
≡

news that upset him /⊙
    passed   said
    e
She past him the potatos and then says, "I saw Sam Fox today. He wasn't
    groaned
limping." ¶"Oh, no!", groans Bryan. "That means he's going to run after all."

B. Proofread the following paragraphs from the same story. There are two spelling errors, one capitalization error, one wrong punctuation mark, and one missing punctuation mark. There are also one mistake in paragraph format and one subject-verb agreement error. Correct the errors.

"Don't let it upset you, Bryan," said his /ather⊙ "Didn't you just beat your
    by
best time buy a minute? Remember all that training!"

    "Yes, Dad, but I still think that I don't have a chance," Bryan replied, shaking
    are
his head.¶Tammy chimed in, "Maybe there is other good runners, but I can already
    e
hear the echos of our cheers as you cross the finish line."

Level 8   Unit 6   Story   *(Use with pupil book pages 227–228.)*
Skill: Students will proofread paragraphs of a story, correcting mistakes in spelling, punctuation, capitalization, and grammar.

Name _____

THE WRITING PROCESS: STORY

RETEACHING WORKBOOK 49

Step 3: Revise

Have I
- made the beginning of the story more interesting?   **yes** ☐
- crossed out any sentences that do not keep to the same point of view? ☐
- added details to make the setting clearer? ☐
- added dialogue, details, and actions to show what the characters are like? ☐

Revise the following paragraphs that begin a story. Use the check list above to help you. Check off each box when you have finished your revision.
- Use the space above each line, on the sides, and below the paragraphs for your changes.
Sample answers:

    The sixty-year-old retired photographer lived alone in a small, tidy
cabin near the Rocky Mountains. Mrs. Wharton loved the peaceful view surrounding
her.
Mrs. Wharton was kind of an interesting person. She lived alone in a nice old house in the country. Whenever I visited her,
    snow-capped mountains around her house.
I enjoyed looking at the beautiful scenery.
    visited, she met me at the path leading to   "Hello!"
The last time I saw her, she came out of her house and said
she shouted   climbed   old, green Volkswagen.
hello as I got out of my car. I'm so glad to see him, she
thought. I wondered why she looked so worried. I followed her
cabin and admired the plain wooden furniture in the compact living room. "How
into her house, which looked the same as always. She told me
well you look, Tony!" she exclaimed. "How are your parents and your sister,
how nice I looked in my new clothes and then asked about my Joanne?"
family. I thanked her and said they were fine. Then I asked how
¶"We're all pretty well, Mrs. Wharton," I replied. "Now, tell me, how are you?"
    "Listen while I tell you why I have asked
she was. She didn't answer. Instead, she told me why she had
you to come," she whispered.
asked me to come.

Level 8   Unit 6   Story   *(Use with pupil book pages 225–226.)*
Skill: Students will revise the beginning of a story, making the beginning more interesting, deleting sentences that do not support the point of view, and adding details, dialogue, and actions.

T24

Name _____

RETEACHING WORKBOOK 51

LANGUAGE AND USAGE

1 | Adjectives

▸ An **adjective** describes, or modifies, a noun or a pronoun.
▸ A **proper adjective** is formed from a proper noun.
▸ **A**, **an**, and **the** are special adjectives called **articles**.
▸ A **predicate adjective** follows a linking verb and describes the subject.

Outerville's rebuilt theater reopened **last** week.
It looked **quaint** and **inviting**.
A local playwright wrote **a new** play for **that** occasion.

Write each word used as an adjective. Include the articles *a*, *an*, and *the*.

Example: The talkative audience entered the quiet theater.
The, talkative, the, quiet

1. A burgundy velvet curtain rose slowly on the lighted stage.
   A, burgundy, velvet, the, lighted

2. Three actors walked onto the set of an ordinary town.
   Three, the, an, ordinary

3. One actor seemed quiet but cheerful. **One, quiet, cheerful**

4. The fascinating story took place in an Iowa town.
   The, fascinating, an, Iowa

5. The actors' costumes were colorful. **The, actors', colorful**

6. A bright, young Asian designer had created ten elegant costumes.
   A, bright, young, Asian, ten, elegant

7. The designer's work added a special touch to this amusing play.
   The, designer's, a, special, this, amusing

8. At the end of the play, twenty pleased players took their bows.
   the, the, twenty, pleased, their

9. The enchanted audience, smiling and appreciative, applauded the actors.
   The, enchanted, smiling, appreciative, the

Level 8 Unit 7 Modifiers (Use with pupil book pages 236–238.)
Skill: Students will identify words used as adjectives.

Name _____

RETEACHING WORKBOOK 52

LANGUAGE AND USAGE

2 | Comparing with Adjectives

▸ The **positive degree** is the basic form of the adjective.
▸ Use the **comparative degree** to compare two things.
▸ Use the **superlative degree** to compare three or more things.
▸ Form the comparative degree with **-er** or **more**.
▸ Form the superlative degree with **-est** or **most**.

Positive Degree	Comparative Degree	Superlative Degree
dirty	dirtier	dirtiest
bad	worse	worst
enjoyable	more enjoyable	most enjoyable

Rewrite each sentence, choosing the correct form of the adjective in parentheses.

Example: The Roeblings built the (more famous, most famous) bridge in New York City.
The Roeblings built the most famous bridge in New York City.

1. When it was completed, the Brooklyn Bridge was the (larger, largest) suspension bridge ever built.
   When it was completed, the Brooklyn Bridge was the largest suspension bridge ever built.

2. Its cables were the (longer, longest) ever used on a suspension bridge.
   Its cables were the longest ever used on a suspension bridge.

3. In 1883 this bridge received (more, most) acclaim than any other bridge.
   In 1883 this bridge received more acclaim than any other bridge.

4. The Brooklyn Bridge is (prettier, prettiest) than many other bridges.
   The Brooklyn Bridge is prettier than many other bridges.

5. Bridges built earlier took (less, fewer) time to construct.
   Bridges built earlier took less time to construct.

6. Of all their creations, the Brooklyn Bridge was the Roeblings' (more impressive, most impressive).
   Of all their creations, the Brooklyn Bridge was the Roeblings' most impressive.

Level 8 Unit 7 Modifiers (Use with pupil book pages 239–241.)
Skill: Students will use the comparative and the superlative forms of adjectives.

UNIT 7 TEACHER'S ANNOTATED PAGES

Name _____

RETEACHING WORKBOOK 53

LANGUAGE AND USAGE

3 | Adverbs

▶ An **adverb** modifies a verb, an adjective, or another adverb.
▶ An adverb tells *how, when, where,* or *to what extent.*
▶ **Intensifiers** are adverbs that tell *to what extent.*

How: The class listened **carefully** to *Gulliver's Travels.*
When: Our teacher **frequently** reads to us from this book.
Where: We stayed **indoors** until the end of the chapter.
To What Extent: The book is **quite** popular with the class.

Write each adverb. Then write the word or words that it modifies.

Example: Jonathan Swift sometimes wrote science fiction.
sometimes—wrote

1. Jonathan Swift wrote quite cleverly about a man named Gulliver.
   quite—cleverly, cleverly—wrote

2. Gulliver traveled first to a land of extremely small people.
   first—traveled, extremely—small

3. Why did he go there?
   Why—did go, there—did go

4. Actually his ship had sunk nearby.
   Actually—had sunk, nearby—had sunk

5. How did Gulliver communicate with these terribly frightened people?
   How—did communicate, terribly—frightened

6. Very quickly Gulliver showed his good intentions.
   Very—quickly, quickly—showed

7. The giant Gulliver soon became rather useful to the tiny people.
   soon—became, rather—useful

8. Later Gulliver had other equally strange adventures.
   Later—had, equally—strange

Level 8 Unit 7 Modifiers   *(Use with pupil book pages 242–244.)*
Skill: Students will identify adverbs and the words that they modify.

Name _____

RETEACHING WORKBOOK 54

LANGUAGE AND USAGE

4 | Comparing with Adverbs

▶ The **positive degree** of an adverb describes one action.
▶ Use the **comparative degree** to compare two actions.
▶ Use the **superlative degree** to compare three or more actions.
▶ Form the comparative degree with *-er* or *more.*
▶ Form the superlative degree with *-est* or *most.*

Positive Degree	Comparative Degree	Superlative Degree
early	earlier	earliest
steadily	more steadily	most steadily
well	better	best

Rewrite each sentence, choosing the correct adverb in parentheses.

Example: The Mt. Baldy hike thrills us (more, most) every year.
The Mt. Baldy hike thrills us more every year.

1. Of all our hikes, the Mt. Baldy hike went (more smoothly, most smoothly).
   Of all our hikes, the Mt. Baldy hike went most smoothly.

2. Samina prepared for the hike (better, best) than any other hiker.
   Samina prepared for the hike better than any other hiker.

3. We started (earlier, earliest) in the morning than we did last year.
   We started earlier in the morning than we did last year.

4. We also walked (farther, further) than we did last year.
   We also walked farther than we did last year.

5. Of all the climbers, Ramon walked (fastest, most fastest).
   Of all the climbers, Ramon walked fastest.

6. We climbed Mt. Baldy (more quickly, most quickly) than we did before.
   We climbed Mt. Baldy more quickly than we did before.

7. With my sturdy boots, I climbed (more easily, most easily) than Dana.
   With my sturdy boots, I climbed more easily than Dana.

8. Of all the hikers, Dana slowed down (less, least) near the top.
   Of all the hikers, Dana slowed down least near the top.

Level 8 Unit 7 Modifiers   *(Use with pupil book pages 245–247.)*
Skill: Students will use the comparative and the superlative forms of adverbs.

T26

Name _____

 RETEACHING WORKBOOK 55

LANGUAGE AND USAGE

5 | Negatives

▶ A **negative** is a word or a contraction that means "no" or "not."
▶ A **double negative** is the incorrect use of two negatives to express one negative idea. Avoid double negatives.

Double Negative: The moon doesn't give off **no** light of its own.
Correct: The moon doesn't give off any light of its own.
Correct: The moon gives off **no** light of its own.

Rewrite each sentence, choosing the correct word or words in parentheses.

Example: The moon isn't (anything, nothing) like the earth.
The moon isn't anything like the earth.

1. The moon (is, isn't) hardly as large as the earth.
   The moon is hardly as large as the earth.

2. Rain doesn't (never, ever) fall on the moon.
   Rain doesn't ever fall on the moon.

3. The moon (has, hasn't) neither an atmosphere nor weather.
   The moon has neither an atmosphere nor weather.

4. Not (anything, nothing) on the moon weighs the same as it does on earth.
   Not anything on the moon weighs the same as it does on earth.

5. I don't believe (any, no) old tales about the moon.
   I don't believe any old tales about the moon.

6. No cow (never, ever) jumped over the moon.
   No cow ever jumped over the moon.

7. There isn't (no, any) green cheese on the moon.
   There isn't any green cheese on the moon.

8. The moon does not follow (nobody, anybody).
   The moon does not follow anybody.

Level 8 Unit 7 Modifiers *(Use with pupil book pages 248–249.)*
Skill: Students will use negatives correctly.

Name _____

 RETEACHING WORKBOOK 56

LANGUAGE AND USAGE

6 | Adjective or Adverb?

▶ Use *good, bad, sure,* and *real* as adjectives.
▶ Use *well, badly, surely,* and *really* as adverbs.
▶ Use *well* as an adjective only when it refers to health.

Adjectives
The scientist's ideas were **good**.
She wasn't **sure** about every invention.
Today her stomach didn't feel **well**.

Adverbs
She studied her notes **well**.
One formula **surely** puzzled her.
An experiment went **badly**.

Rewrite each sentence, choosing the correct adjective or adverb in parentheses.

Example: (Sure, Surely) you've heard about Dr. Strangely's experiments.
Surely you've heard about Dr. Strangely's experiments.

1. Dr. Strangely was a (real, really) amazing scientist.
   Dr. Strangely was a really amazing scientist.

2. This clever scientist (sure, surely) created many new inventions.
   This clever scientist surely created many new inventions.

3. Her inventions weren't (bad, badly); they were different.
   Her inventions weren't bad; they were different.

4. She invented a method of helping people think (good, well).
   She invented a method of helping people think well.

5. Her intentions were always (good, well).
   Her intentions were always good.

6. One invention was for baseball pitchers who had been pitching (bad, badly).
   One invention was for baseball pitchers who had been pitching badly.

7. She hoped that one of her formulas would help sick people feel (good, well).
   She hoped that one of her formulas would help sick people feel well.

8. (Real, Really) quickly, she gained many appreciative customers.
   Really quickly, she gained many appreciative customers.

Level 8 Unit 7 Modifiers *(Use with pupil book pages 250–251.)*
Skill: Students will distinguish between adjectives and adverbs.

Name _____

COMPOSITION SKILL: DESCRIPTION

RETEACHING WORKBOOK 57

Choosing Details

> When you write a description, choose details that suit your purpose and your **point of view**, or attitude.

Read each of these situations. Follow the directions.

A. Here is the way a classified advertisement might describe a dog for sale:

> two-year-old golden retriever, female, gentle; $40

If you call the dog's owners, they will probably tell you more details that they hope will make you want to buy the dog. List four details that would tell you more about the dog and would make you feel you want to buy it.
Sample answers:

1. large, liquid-brown eyes
2. feathery, gold-brown tail
3. greets you at the door
4. likes to be petted

B. You are writing a letter to your cousins in a distant city, asking them to entertain a friend who will be visiting there. List four details so that your cousins will recognize your friend and be glad to meet him or her.

5. short, dark brown hair
6. appears confident
7. small, muscular build
8. friendly smile

C. You have gone away to camp for two weeks and are not having a good time. In a letter to a friend, you tell about things that you don't like. List four details you might include in your letter.

9. mosquitoes biting
10. hard mattresses
11. bugle wakes you up early
12. noisy bunkmates

Level 8 Unit 8 Description (Use with pupil book pages 282–284.)
Skill: Students will write details about people, places, and things that create particular impressions.

Name _____

COMPOSITION SKILL: DESCRIPTION

RETEACHING WORKBOOK 58

Using Descriptive Language

> Use exact adjectives, nouns, verbs, and adverbs, as well as **similes** and **metaphors**, to create vivid pictures in your reader's mind.
>
> **Exact Words:** The athlete leaps aggressively for rebounds.
> **Simile:** The athlete is *like a tightly coiled spring* on the court.
> **Metaphor:** The athlete *is a tiger* when she leaps for rebounds.

Rewrite each sentence, replacing the underlined word or words with more exact words. Use at least one simile and at least one metaphor.
Sample answers:

1. The pretty building was on a nice beach.
   The freshly painted cottage was on a quiet beach.

2. Marty looked tired.
   Marty looked thoroughly exhausted.

3. Jack has a nice smile.
   Jack's smile is like a warm ray of sunshine.

4. The city lights look wonderful from the top of that skyscraper.
   The city lights sparkle brilliantly from the top of that skyscraper.

5. We saw a person go down that slide.
   We saw an excited ten-year-old girl coast down the slick slide.

6. The food smells good.
   The bread smells fragrant and yeasty.

7. Jennifer's voice is nice.
   Jennifer's voice is a clear, sweet bell.

8. He did well.
   He performed the dance gracefully and expressively.

Level 8 Unit 8 Description (Use with pupil book pages 285–287.)
Skill: Students will rewrite sentences, replacing words with more exact words, similes, or metaphors.

UNIT 8 TEACHER'S ANNOTATED PAGES

T28

COMPOSITION SKILL: DESCRIPTION

Organizing Your Description

There are four main ways to organize a description:
1. Use **spatial order**. Organize the details from nearest to farthest, from farthest to nearest; from left to right, from right to left; from top to bottom, or from bottom to top.
2. Start with the detail that strikes you first.
3. Go from the most important detail to the least important detail.
4. Go from the least important detail to the most important detail.

A. List five vivid details to describe what you are wearing. Arrange the details in spatial order from head to toe.

Answers will vary.

_____
_____
_____
_____
_____

B. List five vivid details to describe someone important to you. Start with the least important detail and end with the most important one.

_____
_____
_____
_____
_____

C. List five details about what you see and hear outside your house or apartment building in the morning. Start with the detail that strikes you first.

_____
_____
_____
_____
_____

THE WRITING PROCESS: DESCRIPTION

Step 3: Revise

Have I	yes
added sense words to the description?	☐
added exact words and similes or metaphors to the description?	☐
added details that support the point of view and crossed out any that do not?	☐
changed the order of any sentences that do not fit the organization of the description?	☐

Revise the following story. Use the check list above to help you. Check off each box when you have finished your revision.
- Use a thesaurus to help find exact words.
- Use the space above each line, on the sides, and below the paragraph for your changes.

Sample answers:

was completely involved in basketball

I could tell from Russell's room that he liked sports. By the

an official regulation NBA basketball

door where I walked in was some equipment. Next to that was

Russell's well-worn basketball   Celtics'

a uniform. On the far wall was a sports poster. Between me and

sparkling clean   basketball trophies Russell

the far wall was a shelf full of things the person had won. They

until they shone like mirrors

had been polished and were incredibly shiny. There were books

about monster movies on the shelf too. The lamp under the

basketball! Next to it was a stack of sports

poster was shaped like a piece of sports equipment.

magazines opened to an article about Russell's favorite sport.

Name _____

THE WRITING PROCESS: DESCRIPTION

RETEACHING WORKBOOK 61

Step 4: Proofread

When you proofread, look for mistakes in spelling, capitalization, punctuation, and grammar. Use proofreading marks to make corrections.

Jan's radio is ~~more~~ smaller than mine, but it is really powerful.

Proofreading Marks

⁋ Indent.	∧ Add a comma.	⊙ Add a period.	≡ Capitalize.	❝❞ Add quotation marks.
∧ Add something.	∽ Reverse the order.	⌒ Take out.	/ Make a small letter.	

A. Proofread the following paragraph. There are three spelling errors, two incorrect adjectives, one capitalization error, and one punctuation error. Correct the errors. Use a dictionary to check your spelling.

   best
The ~~better~~ ⋁acation I have ever had was spent at my grandparents' house on the
                        ≡
banks of the Ohio river. When I sat on the porch, I could hear the breeze
                                              t
whispering through the lea~~f~~s of the trees. I lisened to the river. Sometimes it made
                     ve   i
soft lapping noises and other times it made fur~~i~~ous rushing sounds. Grandpa told
                                                                              ly
sailing stories. Of all the sounds, his voice was the most soothing~~est~~.

B. Proofread the following paragraph. There are two spelling errors, one incorrect adjective, one incorrect adverb, one capitalization error, and one punctuation error. Correct the errors.

When you open the door to the Main Street Diner, the smell always rushes out
                                           i   ly
and flows around you. It is a glor~~i~~ous mixture of fresh bread, onions, stew, and
  ve   ⊙
cal~~f~~'s liver. the smell of garlic is real overpowering⌃and it makes all the food more
         ≡
          er
tempting~~er~~⌃than ever.

Level 8 Unit 8 Description (Use with pupil book pages 295–296.)
Skill: Students will proofread paragraphs, correcting mistakes in spelling, capitalization, punctuation, and grammar.

Name _____

MECHANICS

RETEACHING WORKBOOK 63

1 Sentences and Interjections

▶ Every sentence begins with a **capital letter**.
▶ Use a **period** after a declarative or an imperative sentence.
▶ Use a **question mark** after an interrogative sentence.
▶ Use an **exclamation point** after an exclamatory sentence and after an interjection that shows strong feeling.
▶ Use a **comma** after an interjection that shows mild feeling.

Declarative:	My, Stevenson's *Treasure Island* is a great book.
Interrogative:	Have you read this book?
Imperative:	Please take my copy.
Exclamatory:	**Wow!** What an adventure Jim Hawkins had!

Rewrite each sentence, using correct capitalization and end punctuation.

Example: do you like stories about pirates
   Do you like stories about pirates?

1. oh, yes I enjoyed reading *Treasure Island*
   Oh, yes, I enjoyed reading *Treasure Island*.

2. wow what an exciting story it was
   Wow! What an exciting story it was!

3. tell me what happened in the end
   Tell me what happened in the end.

4. no you should read the story yourself
   No, you should read the story yourself.

5. was there really treasure on Treasure Island
   Was there really treasure on Treasure Island?

6. did Jim Hawkins deal with dangerous pirates
   Did Jim Hawkins deal with dangerous pirates?

7. tell me your opinion of the book
   Tell me your opinion of the book.

Level 8 Unit 9 Capitalization and Punctuation (Use with pupil book page 304.)
Skill: Students will capitalize and will punctuate the four types of sentences.

Name _____

RETEACHING WORKBOOK 65

MECHANICS

3 | Uses for Commas

▸ Use a comma to separate items in a series.
▸ Use a comma between two or more adjectives that come before a noun.
▸ Do not use a comma if they express a single idea.
▸ Use a comma to separate simple sentences within a compound sentence.

Terry likes beautiful, solemn music.
She plays music with Ned, Jo, and Ping.
They play in the morning, at night, and on weekends.
Ping plays the piano, Ned sings, and Jo strums the guitar.

Rewrite each sentence, adding commas where they are needed.

Example: Terry has recordings of Mozart Brahms and Bach.
Terry has recordings of Mozart, Brahms, and Bach.

1. Terry loves playing the piano and she loves listening to records.
Terry loves playing the piano, and she loves listening to records.

2. She owns old new and rare recordings.
She owns old, new, and rare recordings.

3. Terry buys records in stores at fairs and at yard sales.
Terry buys records in stores, at fairs, and at yard sales.

4. One record store sells fragile unusual records.
One record store sells fragile, unusual records.

5. The owners keep the old rare recordings in a glass case.
The owners keep the old, rare recordings in a glass case.

6. Terry loves the recordings of Caruso McCormick and Fitzgerald.
Terry loves the recordings of Caruso, McCormick, and Fitzgerald.

7. The record store sells records rents videos and shows films.
The record store sells records, rents videos, and shows films.

8. Terry buys records Ned rents videos and Jo attends films there.
Terry buys records, Ned rents videos, and Jo attends films there.

Level 8 Unit 9 Capitalization and Punctuation *(Use with pupil book pages 308–309.)*
Skill: Students will use commas in a series and in compound sentences.

Name _____

RETEACHING WORKBOOK 64

MECHANICS

2 | Proper Nouns and Proper Adjectives

▸ A proper noun begins with a capital letter.
▸ You can form proper adjectives from proper nouns.
▸ Capitalize proper adjectives.

People: Senator J. Lopez, Uncle Ed   **Languages:** German, Spanish
Places: Gulf of Tonkin, the West   **School Subjects:** Biology 101
Days and Months: Monday, June   **Events:** Civil War
Organizations: National Football League   **Periods of Time:** Dark Ages
Institutions: University of Illinois   **Documents:** Treaty of Paris
Proper Adjectives: French bread, Turkish towel, June wedding

Write each group of words correctly, capitalizing the proper nouns and proper adjectives.

Example: west of ames, iowa   **west of Ames, Iowa**

1. route 3   **Route 3**

2. fourth of july   **Fourth of July**

3. middle ages   **Middle Ages**

4. american canoe association   **American Canoe Association**

5. alma college in michigan   **Alma College in Michigan**

6. a saturday in the spring   **a Saturday in the spring**

7. mrs. canard's french accent   **Mrs. Canard's French accent**

8. boston tea party in 1773   **Boston Tea Party in 1773**

9. sydney opera house in australia   **Sydney Opera House in Australia**

10. death valley in the west   **Death Valley in the West**

11. mom's uncle, uncle jake   **Mom's uncle, Uncle Jake**

12. south of baffin bay   **south of Baffin Bay**

13. idaho potatoes at ted's grocery   **Idaho potatoes at Ted's Grocery**

14. science with dr. amy jurigian   **science with Dr. Amy Jurigian**

15. geology 1 at brown university   **Geology 1 at Brown University**

16. a bengal tiger from india   **a Bengal tiger from India**

Level 8 Unit 9 Capitalization and Punctuation *(Use with pupil book pages 305–307.)*
Skill: Students will capitalize proper nouns and proper adjectives.

T31

UNIT 9 TEACHER'S ANNOTATED PAGES

Name _____

MECHANICS

RETEACHING WORKBOOK 67

5 | Dates, Addresses, and Letters

▶ Use a comma to separate the month and the day from the year.
▶ Use a comma between the city and the state. Use a comma after the state if the address is within the sentence. Use a comma to separate each item except the ZIP Code.
▶ Use a comma after the greeting in friendly letters and after the closing in both friendly and business letters.

Dates and Addresses
July 16, 1990
1002 Madison Avenue
New York, NY 10022

Greetings and Closings
Dear Dinah,
Your sister,
Sincerely yours,

Rewrite the letter, adding commas where they are needed.

122 First Street
Teaneck **,** New Jersey 07666
May 29 **,** 1990

Dear Carmela,

I found the facts that you requested on May 16 **,** 1990 in Chicago **,** Illinois. Woodrow Wilson was born in Staunton **,** Virginia **,** on December 28 **,** 1856. In June 1902 Wilson became president of Princeton University. Later he lived at the White House. That address is 1600 Pennsylvania Avenue **,** Washington **,** D.C. 20013.

Sincerely yours **,**
Stanley

_____

_____

_____

Level 8 Unit 9 Capitalization and Punctuation   (Use with pupil book pages 312–313.)
Skill: Students will use commas in dates and addresses in a letter.

Name _____

MECHANICS

RETEACHING WORKBOOK 66

4 | More Uses for Commas

▶ Use commas after words, phrases, and clauses that come at the beginning of sentences.
▶ Use commas to separate interrupters, nouns of direct address, and unnecessary appositives in a sentence.

Introductory Word: Yes, a musician must have good timing.
Introductory Phrase: Before a piano recital, students practice.
Introductory Clause: While Linda plays, she often composes.
Interrupter: A composer, of course, must have talent.
Noun of Direct Address: Can you read music, Linda?
Appositives: Linda Granges, a composer, arranged this music. She also wrote the song "Willow Tree."

Rewrite each sentence, adding commas where they are needed.

Example: Sue Ling a piano student writes songs as well.
Sue Ling, a piano student, writes songs as well.

1. Say did you know that Sue has written many wonderful songs?
Say, did you know that Sue has written many wonderful songs?

2. Before Sue wrote any songs she listened to a lot of music.
Before Sue wrote any songs, she listened to a lot of music.

3. Linda her song "Soaring" has been recently published.
Linda, her song "Soaring" has been recently published.

4. An ability to read music of course helps musicians.
An ability to read music, of course, helps musicians.

5. During each piano lesson Sue usually takes notes.
During each piano lesson, Sue usually takes notes.

6. Most professional composers study music for a long time you see.
Most professional composers study music for a long time, you see.

7. Sue a serious musician has studied music since she was seven.
Sue, a serious musician, has studied music since she was seven.

Level 8 Unit 9 Capitalization and Punctuation   (Use with pupil book pages 310–311.)
Skill: Students will use commas to set off interrupters and introductory words, phrases, and clauses.

T32

MECHANICS

6 | Quotation Marks

> ▶ Use quotation marks to set off direct quotations from the rest of the sentence.
> ▶ Use quotation marks around the titles of short stories, poems, book chapters, magazine articles, and songs.
> ▶ Capitalize all important words in a title.
>
> **Direct Quotations:** "Deer are lovely animals," said Chen.
> Did Nora say, "I have watched wild deer"?
> **Indirect Quotation:** Nora said that she has photographed deer.
> **Title of a Short Work:** Chen read the article "Deer in the North."

Rewrite each sentence, using correct capitalization and punctuation. The direct quotations are underlined to help you.

Example: Susan said I like deer. _____ Susan said, "I like deer."

1. Chen said male deer grow new antlers each spring.
   Chen said, "Male deer grow new antlers each spring."

2. The article deer move north gives interesting facts about deer.
   The article "Deer Move North" gives interesting facts about deer.

3. Bucks stated Chen have powerful legs.
   "Bucks," stated Chen, "have powerful legs."

4. Deer can run more than thirty miles an hour explained Tony.
   "Deer can run more than thirty miles an hour," explained Tony.

5. Deer can detect motion said Chen. Their sense of smell is sharp.
   "Deer can detect motion," said Chen. "Their sense of smell is sharp."

6. Did Susan say tell me what a deer looks like?
   Did Susan say, "Tell me what a deer looks like"?

7. Chen said that the poem fawn and the story spots are about deer.
   Chen said that the poem "Fawn" and the story "Spots" are about deer.

8. Do deer make sounds asked Susan.
   "Do deer make sounds?" asked Susan.

Level 8 Unit 9 Capitalization and Punctuation (Use with pupil book pages 314–316.)
Skill: Students will capitalize and will punctuate direct quotations and titles of short works.

MECHANICS

7 | Titles of Long Works

> ▶ Underline the titles of major works like books, magazines, news-papers, plays, movies, television series, works of art, and long musical compositions.
> ▶ Capitalize all important words in a title.
>
> My sister's favorite play is Hamlet.
> Monet's The Water Lily Pond is in the Denver Art Museum.
> Our class took a field trip to see the movie The Sound of Music.

Write these titles of long works correctly.

Example: a separate peace _____ A Separate Peace

1. the prince and the pauper
   The Prince and the Pauper

2. symphony no. 3
   Symphony No. 3

3. creative teens
   Creative Teens

4. a raisin in the sun
   A Raisin in the Sun

5. chariots of fire
   Chariots of Fire

6. madam butterfly
   Madam Butterfly

7. usa today
   USA Today

8. portrait of paul revere
   Portrait of Paul Revere

9. the new york times
   The New York Times

10. the once and future king
    The Once and Future King

11. the bill cosby show
    The Bill Cosby Show

12. kitchen still life
    Kitchen Still Life

13. camelot
    Camelot

14. field and stream
    Field and Stream

15. fantasia
    Fantasia

16. the merchant of venice
    The Merchant of Venice

17. the brady bunch
    The Brady Bunch

18. vermont life
    Vermont Life

Level 8 Unit 9 Capitalization and Punctuation (Use with pupil book pages 317–318.)
Skill: Students will capitalize and will punctuate titles of long works.

MECHANICS

8 | **Colons and Semicolons**

> ▶ Use a **colon** after a greeting in a business letter, between the hour and the minutes in time, and before a list.
> ▶ Use a **semicolon** to connect independent clauses that are closely related in thought or that have commas within them.

Colons:	Dear Mr. James**:**
	The practice begins at 6**:**00 P.M.
	Bring the following**:** music, a stand, and your instrument.
Semicolons:	I like this piece**;** Ramon doesn't.
	Di played the music grandly**;** however, she missed some notes.
	Ramon likes jazz, blues, and reggae music**;** and Fran likes classical, rock, and folk music.

Rewrite the part of the letter shown below, adding colons and semicolons where they are needed. The underlined words are clues to help you.

Dear Mrs. Phelps **:**

    I will be at the audition at 5 **:** 00 P.M. I look forward to performing for <u>you</u> **;** I really want to play in your band. I will play these <u>compositions</u> **:** "Billy's Bounce," "Donna Lee," and "Blusette." I usually <u>play</u> jazz, blues, and country <u>however</u>, I play classical music too.

    <u>I</u> understand that your band has four trumpet players, five saxophonists, and four trombone players <u>but</u> I hope you have room for another trumpet player.

Sincerely,
Ashley Palermo

_____

_____

_____

_____

_____

_____

_____

_____

Level 8 Unit 9 Capitalization and Punctuation (Use with pupil book pages 319–320.)
Skill: Students will use colons and semicolons correctly.

T34

MECHANICS

9 | **Abbreviations and Numbers**

> ▶ Most abbreviations begin with a capital letter and end with a period.
> ▶ Spell out numbers under one hundred and numbers at the beginning of a sentence. Use numerals for numbers over one hundred and for sections of writing.

Abbreviations:	Thursday	**Thurs.**	gallon	**gal.**
	Street	**St.**	Senator	**Sen.**
	Corporation	**Corp.**	Post Office	**P.O.**
	Florida	**FL**	American League	**AL**
Numbers:	**Forty-nine** people had voted by **one** o'clock.			
	By **1:55** P.M., **149** people had voted on Question **2**.			

A. Write each phrase, using the correct abbreviation for the underlined word or words. Use your dictionary to help you.

Example: Saturday _____Sat._____

1.	Nick Rose, <u>Senior</u>	**N. Rose, Sr.**	7.	Hays, <u>Kansas</u>	**Hays, KS**
2.	9 <u>miles per hour</u>	**9 mph**	8.	<u>April</u> 1	**Apr. 1**
3.	<u>Forest Service</u>	**FS**	9.	<u>Wednesday</u>	**Wed.**
4.	<u>eight o'clock</u> P.M.	**8:00 P.M.**	10.	2 Ivy <u>Avenue</u>	**2 Ivy Ave.**
5.	Abt <u>Incorporated</u>	**Abt Inc.**	11.	<u>Apartment</u> 7	**Apt. 7**
6.	River <u>High School</u>	**River H.S.**	12.	11 <u>inches</u>	**11 in.**

B. Rewrite each sentence, correcting the underlined words and numerals.

13. At <u>one-fifty</u> the plane from Dallas arrived with <u>200</u> passengers.
    At 1:50 the plane from Dallas arrived with two hundred passengers.

14. <u>1</u> passenger waved from Gate <u>Six</u> to her waiting family.
    One passenger waved from Gate 6 to her waiting family.

15. At 2 o'clock <u>51</u> people boarded the airplane.
    At two o'clock fifty-one people boarded the airplane.

16. The plane left at <u>two-ten</u> P.M. with <u>two hundred fifty-one</u> passengers.
    The plane left at 2:10 P.M. with 251 passengers.

Name _____

 RETEACHING WORKBOOK

MECHANICS

11 | Hyphens, Dashes, and Parentheses

- Use a **hyphen** to divide a word at the end of a line, to join the parts of compound numbers, and to join two or more words that work together as one adjective before a noun.
- Use **dashes** to show a sudden change of thought.
- Use **parentheses** to enclose unnecessary information.

Hyphens: forty-two, two-thirds full, well-deserved praise
Dash: Tim lit the wood stove—Ben Franklin's invention.
Parentheses: Ben Franklin (1706–1790) experimented with electricity. Franklin (the inventor) became ambassador to France.

A. Rewrite the sentences, adding hyphens and dashes where they are needed. The underlined words are clues to help you.

Example: He lived eighty four years. ____ He lived eighty-four years.

1. Benjamin Franklin he was a founding father of his country invented many well known items.
   Benjamin Franklin—he was a founding father of his country—invented many well-known items.

2. He was one third statesman, one third writer, and one third inventor.
   He was one-third statesman, one-third writer, and one-third inventor.

3. At age eighty one he lived a long life Franklin still actively served his country.
   At age eighty-one—he lived a long life—Franklin still actively served his country.

B. Rewrite the sentences, adding parentheses where they are needed. Use the underlined words to help you.

4. Ts'ai Lun a Chinese official invented paper in about A.D. 105.
   Ts'ai Lun (a Chinese official) invented paper in about A.D. 105.

5. The cotton gin invented by Eli Whitney removes seeds from cotton.
   The cotton gin (invented by Eli Whitney) removes seeds from cotton.

6. Thomas Edison 1847–1931 improved the electric light bulb.
   Thomas Edison (1847–1931) improved the electric light bulb.

Level 8 Unit 9 Capitalization and Punctuation (Use with pupil book pages 326–327.)
Skill: Students will use hyphens, dashes, and parentheses correctly.

Name _____

 RETEACHING WORKBOOK

MECHANICS

10 | Apostrophes

- Add an **apostrophe** and **s** to singular nouns and to plural nouns not ending in **s** to show possession. Add an apostrophe to plural nouns ending in **s** to show possession.
- Add an apostrophe and **s** to form the plural of letters, numerals, symbols, and words that refer to themselves. Use an apostrophe in contractions.

Possessive Nouns: senator's, Smith's, children's, classmates'
Contractions: didn't, wouldn't, they're, we'll
Plurals of Letters, Numerals, and Symbols: A's and B's, 6's, t's, %'s
Plurals of Names of Words: and's, good's, remember's

Rewrite the sentences, adding apostrophes where they are needed. The underlined words and symbols are clues to help you.

Example: Bridgets almanac is blue. ____ Bridget's almanac is blue.

1. Janiss almanac has a section on the Olympics.
   Janis's almanac has a section on the Olympics.

2. One gymnast in the last Olympics received five 10s.
   One gymnast in the last Olympics received five 10's.

3. There are six *s on this list of gold medal winners.
   There are six *'s on this list of gold medal winners.

4. Ingemar Stenmarks medal was for the mens slalom.
   Ingemar Stenmark's medal was for the men's slalom.

5. On the list are five gymnasts with two ss in their names.
   On the list are five gymnasts with two s's in their names.

6. My two sisters teacher wants world population figures.
   My two sisters' teacher wants world population figures.

7. The *Norths* and the *Souths* are incorrectly placed on this map.
   The *North's* and the *South's* are incorrectly placed on this map.

8. Theyll confuse many readers. ____ **They'll confuse many readers.**

Level 8 Unit 9 Capitalization and Punctuation (Use with pupil book pages 324–325.)
Skill: Students will use apostrophes correctly in possessive nouns, contractions, and plurals.

Name _____

COMPOSITION SKILL: PERSUASIVE LETTER — RETEACHING WORKBOOK 75

Writing Business Letters

> **A business letter** is a formal letter written for a purpose, such as to apply for a job, to order something, to request information, or to complain about a product or a service. The letter should be polite and to the point and should include all necessary information. A business letter has six parts: heading, inside address, greeting, body, closing, and signature. The greeting is followed by a colon (:). Write a business letter in block or modified block style.

Write a business letter to the president of Business Bank of Bethel at 427 Lake Avenue in Bethel, Maine 04217. Tell the president that you are interested in starting a bike messenger service. Ask for information about starting and managing a small business. Use your own name and address and today's date.

Answers will vary.

_____
_____
_____
_____
_____
_____
_____
_____
_____
_____
_____
_____
_____
_____
_____
_____

Level 8 Unit 10 Persuasive Letter *(Use with pupil book pages 357–359.)*
Skill: Students will write a business letter, requesting information.

Name _____

COMPOSITION SKILL: PERSUASIVE LETTER — RETEACHING WORKBOOK 76

Stating and Supporting an Opinion

> When you write to persuade, state your opinion clearly and support it with reasons and factual examples. Suit your reasons to your audience.

A. Imagine that you are a salesperson at the Viper-1 car dealership. Below are some possible reasons you could use to support the opinion *You should buy a Viper-1 car.* Underline the reason that best answers each question below.

1. Which of the following reasons would best persuade a customer with four children?
   a. The Viper-1 has a four-speed transmission and fuel injection.
   b. The Viper-1 has hand-tooled leather seats and walnut paneling.
   <u>c. The Viper-1 seats six and has a huge trunk.</u>

2. Which of the following reasons is not related to the opinion?
   <u>a. The Viper-1 commercials are some of the best on TV.</u>
   b. The Viper-1 offers a five-year guarantee.
   c. The Viper-1 averages forty miles per gallon of gas.

3. Which of the following is a provable fact?
   <u>a. The Viper-1 was named Car of the Year by *Car Critic* magazine.</u>
   b. The Viper-1 gives the most comfortable ride of any car on the road.
   c. The Viper factory employs only the best engineers and mechanics.

4. Which of the following reasons is stated most strongly and clearly?
   a. The buyers I've talked with seem content with their Viper-1 cars.
   <u>b. We've sold six hundred Viper-1 cars this year without a single complaint.</u>
   c. You'll probably like the Viper-1 a lot once you get used to it.

B. Read the following paragraph. Underline the opinion. Then list three supporting reasons.

<u>I think our club dues should be put in a savings account.</u> Our dues would then earn interest, which would give us more money to spend later. It would also be safer in a bank than in a cracker tin in an unlocked room. If the money is easy for us to get, we would be more likely to spend it and less likely to save it. A savings account makes good business sense to me! **Sample answers:**

Interest from dues would give us more spending money.

Money would be safer in a bank.

We would spend money instead of save it if it is easy to get it.

Level 8 Unit 10 Persuasive Letter *(Use with pupil book pages 361–362.)*
Skill: Students will identify reasons that fit given standards and will identify an opinion and supporting reasons in a persuasive letter.

UNIT 10 TEACHER'S ANNOTATED PAGES

T36

Using Persuasive Strategies

When you have an opinion and reasons that support it, use these persuasive strategies in your argument.

Offer a precedent, or refer to a similar situation as an example.
Appeal to fairness with a solid example.
Overcome objections by answering them before they are raised.
Explore consequences by naming good results your idea might have and overcoming unfavorable results.

Read the following part of a letter written to support the opinion stated in the first paragraph. Look for persuasive strategies. Then use the sentences from the letter to answer the questions below.

Dear Editor:

The legal driving age should be fifteen. Here are my reasons.

The present law concerning the age limit was made when teen-agers had few places to go. Driving is more important now, and I think it is only fair to reconsider the age limit.

I know that fourteen-year-olds lack experience. However, they would quickly gain it. Younger drivers also have better eyesight and reflexes than older drivers.

When cars were first being driven, there were no age limits for drivers. Many teen-agers drove. There were also far fewer accidents in those days.

Driving would allow young people to see more of the world. They also could help their parents by doing chores that demand a car.

Sincerely,

Mort Simmons

1. Which sentence offers a precedent? **When cars were first being driven, there were no age limits for drivers.**

2. Which sentence appeals to fairness? **The present law concerning the age limit was made when teen-agers had few places to go.**

3. Which sentence overcomes an objection? **I know that fourteen-year-olds lack experience.**

4. Which sentence explores consequences? **Driving would allow young people to see more of the world.**

Shaping Your Argument

Begin a persuasive paragraph with a clear topic sentence. Support your opinion with reasons arranged in an **order of importance** that will suit your audience. The order may be from most to least important or from least to most important. Finish with a strong summary statement.

A. Suppose that you have just learned about a new football helmet. You want to convince your coach to let your team try these new helmets. Place a check beside the sentence or sentences that answer each question below.

1. Which topic sentence states the opinion more clearly?

   a. ✓ Kango helmets can help our team in more ways than one.

   b. _____ You should look at this new line of helmets.

2. Which three reasons below would be most likely to convince a coach?

   a. ✓ Kangoes weigh half as much as ordinary helmets.

   b. _____ Kangoes are made by a European company that once made knight's armor.

   c. _____ Kangoes cost a little more than ordinary helmets.

   d. ✓ Kangoes reduce head and neck injuries by eighty per cent.

   e. ✓ Kangoes feature a new design with a permanent, scratch-proof finish.

3. Which is the stronger summary statement?

   a. _____ As you can see, the new Kango helmets are quite attractive.

   b. ✓ A Kango helmet is a winner in performance and safety.

B. Using your choices above, write a paragraph to persuade your coach to try Kango helmets. Write your supporting reasons in least to most important order.

Kango helmets can help our team in more ways than one. Kangoes feature a new design with a permanent, scratch-proof finish. Kangoes weigh half as much as ordinary helmets. Kangoes reduce head and neck injuries by eighty per cent. A Kango helmet is a winner in performance and safety.

Name _____

THE WRITING PROCESS: PERSUASIVE LETTER

RETEACHING WORKBOOK 79

Step 3: Revise

Have I	yes
added a topic sentence that clearly states the opinion?	☐
added supporting reasons and specific examples, including a reason that overcomes an objection or that offers a precedent?	☐
crossed out reasons that are weak or not relevant and checked that supporting reasons are in a convincing order?	☐
added a concluding statement that emphasizes or restates the opinion?	☐

Revise the following persuasive letter. Use the check list above to help you. Check off each box when you have finished your revision.
• Use the space above each line, on the sides, and below the paragraph for your changes.
Sample answers:

Dear Mr. Pick:

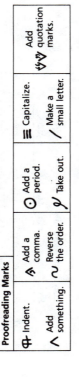

I want to study with the best guitar teacher in town. You don't know me, but I'm writing to you anyway. I've heard a lot about you. My friend Carla Rizzo, a student of yours, says that you're the best guitar teacher. I want to take lessons. I have my own guitar and have been playing for a while more than two years on my own. I hope to be a professional musician someday. If That is why I feel that it's so important for me to have the best teacher. not, maybe I will work as an artist or in the computer field. I can't afford to pay much, but Carla says that you sometimes lower your rates for good students. I'll work hard. If you accept me as a student, I'll do my best to make you proud! Carla told me that you're not accepting any more new students. However, I hope you'll make an exception for me, since I have proved my dedication to music. I have also taken piano lessons for three years and have never missed a lesson or a day of practice.

Level 8 Unit 10 Persuasive Letter (Use with pupil book pages 369–370.)
Skill: Students will revise a persuasive letter, adding a topic sentence, supporting reasons, and specific examples, checking that reasons are relevant and in order, and adding a concluding statement.

Name _____

THE WRITING PROCESS: PERSUASIVE LETTER

RETEACHING WORKBOOK 80

Step 4: Proofread

When you proofread, look for mistakes in spelling, capitalization, and punctuation. Use proofreading marks to make corrections.

please put me on your Mailing list i want to receive pamphlets on water safety.

Proofreading Marks

¶ Indent.	∧ Add a comma.	≡ Capitalize.
∧ Add something.	∽ Reverse the order.	/ Make a small letter.
	⊙ Add a period.	∨∨ Add quotation marks.
	⌿ Take out.	

Proofread this business letter. There are two spelling errors, four capitalization errors, four punctuation errors, one incorrectly written number, and two errors in abbreviation. Correct the errors. Use a dictionary to check your spelling.

70 Tumbleweed road
Cave Creek AZ 85331
August 2, 1990

Oceans Unlimited, Inc
101 Coral drive
Alturas FL 33820

Dear Sir or madam:

This is in response to your ad in the july issue of Splash magazine.
scuba   50.00
Please send me the s.c.u.b.d. outfit advertised. I am enclosing the $ fifty
shipping cost required. I understand that the balance of $315.00 is to be paid
                     ac
COD. I except this arrangement.

Level 8 Unit 10 Persuasive Letter (Use with pupil book pages 371–372.)
Skill: Students will proofread a business letter, correcting mistakes in spelling, capitalization, and punctuation.

Name _____

RETEACHING WORKBOOK 81

LANGUAGE AND USAGE

1 Personal and Possessive Pronouns

▶ A **pronoun** is used to replace a noun.
▶ **Personal pronouns** have different forms to show person, number, and gender.
▶ A **possessive pronoun** can replace a possessive noun.

	first	second	third
Person:	I like sewing.	You like singing.	They like painting.
	singular		plural
Number:	Marcia teaches **him**.		Marcia teaches **them**.
	masculine	feminine	neuter
Gender:	**He** is a sculptor.	**She** is a sculptor.	**It** is a sculpture.

Possessive: The class admires **her** work. That design is **hers**.

A. Label each underlined pronoun *first person, second person,* or *third person.* Then label it *singular* or *plural.*

Example: Ms. Gray teaches us silk-screening.   **first person, plural**

1. We make prints on paper and cloth.   **first person, plural**
2. Do you two like the designs?   **second person, plural**
3. Please help me prepare two screens.   **first person, singular**
4. They are usually made of silk.   **third person, plural**
5. It is a fascinating printing technique.   **third person, singular**
6. Sid, would you like to join the class?   **second person, singular**
7. Marcia can show him how to begin.   **third person, singular**
8. She is a good teacher and artist.   **third person, singular**

B. Write the correct word in parentheses to complete each sentence.

Example: Do you like **your** Saturday class? (your, you're)

9. The class is having **its** first art show. (it's, its)
10. The students created **their** own designs. (their, they're)
11. Amanda is exhibiting **her** prints. (her, hers)
12. Cassie is exhibiting **hers** too. (her, hers)
13. The prints in the corner are **theirs**. (there's, theirs)
14. **Mine** are the ones by the window. (My, Mine)

Level 8 Unit 11 Pronouns   *(Use with pupil book pages 380–382.)*
Skill: Students will identify the person and number of personal pronouns and will use possessive pronouns correctly.

T39

Name _____

RETEACHING WORKBOOK 82

LANGUAGE AND USAGE

2 Pronoun Antecedents

▶ An **antecedent** is a noun or a pronoun to which a pronoun refers.
▶ A pronoun must agree with its antecedent in person, number, and gender.

People applauded. **They** were ready to enjoy the play.
They grew quiet, and an announcer welcomed **them**.
Although **it** was simple, the set was beautiful.
Both the star and the minor characters knew **their** parts.
Would the stage manager or the prompters forget **their** jobs?

A. Complete each sentence, using the pronoun that agrees with the underlined antecedent or antecedents.

Example: The actors gave **their** best performance. (her, their)

1. Sarah Bernhardt was a famous French actress. Thousands of fans admired **her**. (them, her)
2. Sarah had talent and beauty, and **they** drew praise from the critics. (it, they)
3. Did Sarah or other performers of the time use **their** talents in movies as well? (her, their)

B. Rewrite the sentences so that the antecedents of the underlined pronouns are clear. **Sample answers:**

Example: They followed Sarah's career for sixty years.
             Fans followed Sarah's career for sixty years.

4. When she was on stage, Sarah made it seem so easy.
   When she was on stage, Sarah made acting seem so easy.
5. They say that Sarah could have played any role well.
   Critics say that Sarah could have played any role well.
6. My grandmother saw Sarah Bernhardt perform when she was a girl.
   My grandmother saw Sarah Bernhardt perform when Grandma was a girl.

Level 8 Unit 11 Pronouns   *(Use with pupil book pages 383–385.)*
Skill: Students will choose pronouns to agree with their antecedents and will correct sentences with unclear antecedents.

Name _____

RETEACHING WORKBOOK 83

LANGUAGE AND USAGE

3 | Pronoun Case

- Subject pronouns are in the **nominative case**.
- Use the nominative case for pronouns used as subjects and predicate pronouns.
- Object pronouns are in the **objective case**.
- Use the objective case for pronouns used as direct objects and indirect objects.

                    subject
Nominative: My friends and **I** admire Anna Pavlova's career.
                  predicate pronoun
        Our favorite dancer is **she**.
                         direct object
Objective: Pavlova's career fascinates **us**.
             indirect object   indirect object
      Please lend **her** and **me** the book about Pavlova.

Write the correct pronoun forms in parentheses to complete these sentences.

Example: Carmen and (I, me) saw a film about Anna Pavlova.   __I__

1. The film inspired her and (I, me).   __me__
2. (She, Her) and I both study ballet.   __She__
3. It is (she, her) who has studied the longest.   __she__
4. (We, Us) and the other students in our class work hard.   __We__
5. Mr. Armado teaches (they, them) and (we, us) difficult steps.   __them, us__
6. It was (he, him) who suggested the film about Pavlova.   __he__
7. Great challenges faced (she, her).   __her__
8. Pavlova never gave (they, them) a chance to discourage her.   __them__
9. (She, Her) and her partners practiced constantly.   __She__
10. Pavlova and (they, them) could not depend upon talent alone.   __they__
11. Mr. Armado is strict, but now we appreciate (he, him) more.   __him__
12. The people in need of the most practice are (we, us).   __we__

Level 8   Unit 11   Pronouns   *(Use with pupil book pages 386–388.)*
Skill: Students will choose pronouns in the nominative and the objective cases to complete sentences.

Name _____

RETEACHING WORKBOOK 84

LANGUAGE AND USAGE

4 | Interrogative Pronouns

- **Interrogative pronouns** like *who, which, what, whom,* and *whose* ask questions.
- Use *who* as a subject, *whom* as an object, and *whose* as a possessive.
- Do not confuse the pronoun *whose* with the contraction *who's*.

    Who are the reporters?   **Whom** are they following?
    Whose is that uniform?   **Who's** the pilot?

Complete each sentence, using the correct word in parentheses.

Example: __Who__ is Sally Ride? (Who, Whom)

1. __Who__ are the other astronauts? (Who, Whom)
2. __Whom__ did the President meet? (Who, Whom)
3. __Which__ is the spacecraft to be launched? (Which, Whom)
4. __Whose__ is that silver helmet? (Who's, Whose)
5. __Who's__ checking the spacecraft? (Who's, Whose)
6. __What__ was the problem? (What, Whom)
7. __Who__ is the youngest astronaut? (Who, Whom)
8. __Whose__ are the most demanding roles on board? (Who's, Whose)
9. __Whom__ did the reporters interview? (Who, Whom)
10. __Who's__ had the most experience in space? (Who's, Whose)
11. __What__ will this mission accomplish? (What, Who)
12. __Who__ was chosen to leave the space capsule? (Who, Whom)
13. __Whom__ can the astronauts contact on Earth? (Who, Whom)
14. __Which__ was the longest space flight? (Which, Whom)
15. __Whose__ is that voice on the loudspeaker? (Who's, Whose)
16. __Who__ decides the purpose of the flight? (Who, Whom)
17. __Who's__ taking photographs of the liftoff? (Who's, Whose)
18. __Whom__ should we ask for more information? (Who, Whom)

Level 8   Unit 11   Pronouns   *(Use with pupil book pages 389–390.)*
Skill: Students will use interrogative pronouns and *who's* correctly.

LANGUAGE AND USAGE

5 | Demonstrative Pronouns

▶ A **demonstrative pronoun** points out persons, places, things, or ideas.
▶ *This* and *that* refer to singular nouns or pronouns.
▶ *These* and *those* refer to plural nouns or pronouns.
▶ *This* and *these* point out things that are close.
▶ *That* and *those* point out things that are farther away.

This is a double-decker bus.   **These** are double-decker buses.
That is a bus across the street.   **Those** are the buses over there.

Rewrite the sentences, using the correct words in parentheses.

Example: (This, These) is the city of London.

This is the city of London.

1. Are (this, these) the maps of the city?
    Are these the maps of the city?

2. (This, That) looks like Big Ben right here.
    This looks like Big Ben right here.

3. (That, Those) are the hedges surrounding Kensington Park.
    Those are the hedges surrounding Kensington Park.

4. Isn't (this, that) Buckingham Palace across the park?
    Isn't that Buckingham Palace across the park?

5. (These here, These) are tourists hoping to see the queen.
    These are tourists hoping to see the queen.

6. (This, These) is the entrance to the underground.
    This is the entrance to the underground.

7. (That there, That) is our train to the West End.
    That is our train to the West End.

8. (Those there, Those) are the famous West End statues.
    Those are the famous West End statues.

LANGUAGE AND USAGE

6 | Indefinite Pronouns

▶ An **indefinite pronoun** does not refer to a specific person or thing.
▶ Verbs must agree in number with indefinite pronouns used as subjects. Pronouns must agree with indefinite pronouns used as antecedents.

Singular: **Everyone** is reading the same science book.
                Most of the book has interesting information in it.
Plural: **Several** of the students use the book on field trips.
                Most of my classmates take the book with them on the trips.

Rewrite each sentence, using the word in parentheses that agrees with the underlined indefinite pronoun.

Example: Many of the exhibits (sounds, sound) interesting.

Many of the exhibits sound interesting.

1. Everybody (thinks, think) that the science trips are very good.
    Everybody thinks that the science trips are very good.

2. Many of us (looks, look) forward to these trips.
    Many of us look forward to these trips.

3. Some of the information is new, and students take notes on (it, them).
    Some of the information is new, and students take notes on it.

4. Someone (is, are) now organizing a trip to the Botanical Gardens.
    Someone is now organizing a trip to the Botanical Gardens.

5. Most of the rocks there have fossil plants and animals in (it, them).
    Most of the rocks there have fossil plants and animals in them.

6. Both of the eighth grade science classes (plans, plan) to go.
    Both of the eighth grade science classes plan to go.

7. Nobody in the eighth grade (has, have) ever seen a botanical garden.
    Nobody in the eighth grade has ever seen a botanical garden.

8. Each of our trips has had (its, their) own special attraction.
    Each of our trips has had its own special attraction.

Name _____

RETEACHING WORKBOOK 87

LANGUAGE AND USAGE

7 | Reflexive and Intensive Pronouns

▶ A **reflexive pronoun** ends in *-self* or *-selves* and refers to the subject of the sentence. It generally cannot be left out of the sentence.
▶ An **intensive pronoun** ends in *-self* or *-selves* and emphasizes another word in the sentence. Avoid using pronouns with *-self* or *-selves* as personal pronouns.

Reflexive: Maria made **herself** a printing block.
Intensive: The block **itself** was very interesting.

Rewrite each sentence, using the correct pronoun in parentheses.

Example: I found (me, myself) looking at some greeting cards.
I found myself looking at some greeting cards.

1. Mario designed these greeting cards (hisself, himself).
Mario designed these greeting cards himself.

2. He gave (me, myself) a copy of each one.
He gave me a copy of each one.

3. Several of us taught (us, ourselves) how to make printing blocks.
Several of us taught ourselves how to make printing blocks.

4. You might want to try it (yourself, yourselves), Robby.
You might want to try it yourself, Robby.

5. When the project began, I asked (me, myself) if I would complete it.
When the project began, I asked myself if I would complete it.

6. Mario and (I, myself) have a new idea for a design.
Mario and I have a new idea for a design.

7. I (me, myself) prefer to do the actual carving of the block.
I myself prefer to do the actual carving of the block.

8. The carved blocks (theirselves, themselves) are very attractive.
The carved blocks themselves are very attractive.

Level 8 Unit 11 Pronouns *(Use with pupil book pages 397–399.)*
Skill: Students will use reflexive pronouns, intensive pronouns, and personal pronouns correctly.

Name _____

RETEACHING WORKBOOK 88

LANGUAGE AND USAGE

8 | Choosing the Right Pronoun

▶ If you use *we* or *us* with a noun, use the pronoun case that you would use if the noun were not there.
▶ To decide which pronoun form to use in an incomplete comparison, add words to complete the comparison.

We students are working hard.   *(We are working hard.)*
Nobody disturbs **us** students in the library.   *(Nobody disturbs us.)*
I like the work more than **he.**   *(I like the work more than he does.)*
I like the work more than **him.**   *(I like the work more than I like him.)*

Rewrite each sentence, using the correct pronoun in parentheses.

Example: Ernie is a harder worker than (he, him).
Ernie is a harder worker than he.

1. Exam time always affects (we, us) students.
Exam time always affects us students.

2. (We, Us) students really must get to work.
We students really must get to work.

3. Nobody knows that more than (I, me).
Nobody knows that more than I.

4. Kira always does better on her exams than (I, me).
Kira always does better on her exams than I.

5. (We, Us) eighth graders have to study harder than the seventh graders.
We eighth graders have to study harder than the seventh graders.

6. More time is given them than (we, us).
More time is given them than us.

7. Ms. LaPlace is giving (we, us) French students special help.
Ms. LaPlace is giving us French students special help.

8. Last year the German students had much higher scores than (we, us).
Last year the German students had much higher scores than we.

Level 8 Unit 11 Pronouns *(Use with pupil book pages 400–401.)*
Skill: Students will use pronouns with nouns and in incomplete comparisons.

UNIT 11   TEACHER'S ANNOTATED PAGES

T42

Name _____

COMPOSITION SKILL: RESEARCH REPORT

Finding and Narrowing a Topic

Before you write a report, find a topic that really interests you and that will interest your readers. Be sure that you can find information on the topic easily and that it is narrow enough for a short report. Narrow your topic by choosing just one aspect of it or by asking questions about it until you narrow the topic to what interests you most.

Put a check next to the topic in each group that is narrow enough for a short report. Then, for each group, write a topic of your own that is narrow enough for a short report.

1. _____ American movies

   _____ Movies

   ✓ Some famous American science-fiction movies of the 1950s

   Narrowed Topic: **Answers will vary.**

2. _____ Different types of storms

   ✓ How a hurricane forms

   _____ Types of weather

   Narrowed Topic: _____

3. _____ Great mountains of the world

   _____ Mount Everest

   ✓ The first successful climb of Mount Everest

   Narrowed Topic: _____

4. ✓ A day in the life of a Japanese high-school student

   _____ What high schools are like in different countries of the world

   _____ Schools throughout history

   Narrowed Topic: _____

5. _____ Classic American cars

   ✓ The Model T—a classic American car

   _____ Classic cars around the world

   Narrowed Topic: _____

Level 8 Unit 12 Research Report (Use with pupil book pages 432–433.)
Skill: Students will identify topics narrow enough for short reports and will write narrowed topics of their own.

Name _____

COMPOSITION SKILL: RESEARCH REPORT

Planning and Researching a Report

Plan your report by first asking yourself what you want to know about your topic and then looking for the answers in appropriate reference sources.

An **encyclopedia** contains articles on many subjects. An **atlas** contains maps and tables that show population and geographical information. An **almanac** contains up-to-date information on many subjects. A **dictionary** contains not only words but also biographical and geographical information. A **biographical reference book** contains information about people. The *Readers' Guide to Periodical Literature* lists articles published in periodicals. A **nonfiction book** is a factual book on a subject. A **newspaper** contains news stories on current topics.

Write *encyclopedia, atlas, almanac, dictionary, biographical reference, Readers' Guide, nonfiction book,* or *newspaper* to tell where you would look for the answer to each of the following questions.

Sample answers:

1. Is Rome, Italy, near the mountains or near the sea? **atlas**

2. When was the first piano made? **encyclopedia**

3. How many people live in France? **almanac**

4. When did Hank Aaron set his home-run record? **almanac**

5. What recent articles discuss Halley's comet? **Readers' Guide**

6. What does a lute look like? **dictionary or encyclopedia**

7. Where did writer Nikki Giovanni grow up? **biographical reference**

8. How are tunnels built? **encyclopedia or nonfiction book**

9. What are the latest published data on cancer research? **Readers' Guide**

10. What are the habits of the gnu? **encyclopedia or nonfiction book**

11. What major highway connects Hartford and Boston? **atlas**

12. What profession paid the highest average salary last year? **almanac**

13. How many feet are there in a kilometer? **dictionary or encyclopedia**

14. Who was Mary Pickford? **encyclopedia or biographical reference**

15. What was Lucille Ball's childhood like? **nonfiction book**

16. Who was elected to the United States Senate yesterday? **newspaper**

Level 8 Unit 12 Research Report (Use with pupil book pages 434–436.)
Skill: Students will identify the best reference source to find a particular type of information.

Name _____

COMPOSITION SKILL: RESEARCH REPORT

RETEACHING WORKBOOK 91

Taking Notes

> Before you start taking notes, make a list of questions you would like to answer. As you read, look for the answers to your questions. Write each question on a separate note card, and then write brief answers in your own words, based on what you have read.

Read the following paragraphs. Take notes below to answer the question *Besides management of timber resources, what does a forester do?*

In addition to the careful harvesting, planting, and breeding of timber resources, foresters have other jobs. One of these jobs concerns water. Forests are known as *watersheds*. The soil of a forest is porous and allows water from rain and snow to enter the ground and gradually pass into springs, streams, and rivers. Foresters keep the soil porous by planting trees and shrubs in bare areas. They also regulate the grazing of livestock. Overgrazing can damage watersheds.

Just as it is important to keep a balance of trees in the forest, a balance of wildlife is necessary. Squirrels and birds can live in tall trees, but ground animals need bushes and shrubs to survive. Foresters clear areas of tall trees to permit the growth of low plants. They intentionally leave hollow logs as potential homes for animals.

Most foresters are best known for being fire spotters and firefighters. However, there are times when foresters start fires. This type of fire is called *prescribed burning*. Foresters start these small fires in order to eliminate some of the brush that may fuel a real fire. **Sample answers:**

—**plants trees and shrubs to keep soil porous**

—**regulates the grazing of livestock**

—**preserves wildlife by creating homes**

—**acts as fire spotter and firefighter**

—**eliminates possible fuel for fire by prescribed burning**

Level 8 Unit 12 Research Report (*Use with pupil book pages 437–438.*)
Skill: Students will read a selection and will take notes to answer a question about it.

Name _____

COMPOSITION SKILL: RESEARCH REPORT

RETEACHING WORKBOOK 92

Making an Outline

> Organize the information from your notes in an outline. **Main topics** are the main ideas that are based on the questions you wrote. Main topics are placed after Roman numerals. **Subtopics** are the facts that support the main topics. They are placed after capital letters. **Details** are specific facts or examples that tell about the subtopics. They are placed after numbers.

Use these notes to complete the outline below. Turn the questions into main topics. Write the supporting facts as subtopics. Write the facts that tell about the subtopics as details.

What kinds of foods will be on a space shuttle?
—dehydrated foods
—dehydrated foods such as fruits, vegetables, cereals
—canned foods

What is a description of the space suit worn outside the shuttle?
—inflatable basic layer to maintain pressure
—restraint layer to keep basic layer from ballooning
—fireproof layers for protection
—built-in backpack containing necessities
Sample answers:

Life in a Space Shuttle

I. **Foods that will be on a space shuttle**
   A. **Dehydrated foods**
      1. **Fruits**
      2. **Vegetables**
      3. **Cereals**
   B. **Canned foods**

II. **Description of the space suit worn outside the shuttle**
   A. **Inflatable basic layer to maintain pressure**
   B. **Restraint layer to keep basic layer from ballooning**
   C. **Fireproof layers for protection**
   D. **Built-in backpack containing necessities**

Level 8 Unit 12 Research Report (*Use with pupil book pages 439–440.*)
Skill: Students will complete an outline from notes.

Writing Introductions and Conclusions

Begin every report with an **introduction** and end it with a **conclusion**.
Write an introduction that captures your reader's interest. Include a sentence that tells exactly what the report is about. Write a conclusion that restates the main ideas and may also review the main points. For a short report, the introduction and conclusion are usually a paragraph each.

Read the following short report. Then rewrite the introductory paragraph and the concluding paragraph so that each one is better.

Bees can communicate with each other. I am going to tell you how they do it. It's really interesting.

Through various ''dances'' a bee can tell other bees the precise direction and distance of food from the hive. The circle dance tells that the food is within a hundred yards. The waggle dance, in which the bee moves in a figure eight, tells that the food is farther away. The speed of the waggle dance indicates how much farther. The faster the bee dances, the closer the food is to the hive.

During the waggle dance, the dancer indicates in which direction the bees must fly to find the food. The dancer crosses from one loop of the eight to the other in the direction of the food.

This is how bees communicate. It's kind of amazing, really, when you think about it.

Introduction: Answers will vary. _____

_____

_____

_____

_____

_____

Conclusion: _____

_____

_____

_____

_____

_____

Level 8   Unit 12   Research Report   *(Use with pupil book pages 440–441.)*
Skill: Students will rewrite the introduction and the conclusion of a report.

Making Transitions

When you write, connect sentences and paragraphs with transition words and phrases. Use transition words and phrases in the following ways.

To introduce examples: for example, for instance, to illustrate, in fact
To add another point: in addition, also, furthermore, a second
To show time relationships: finally, before, after, then, eventually
To signal results or effects: as a result, therefore, for this reason
To show comparison or contrast: similarly, just as, on the other hand
To connect ideas: yet, however, though, so, nevertheless, moreover

In each pair of sentences below, a transition word or phrase is missing. Decide what purpose the transition should have in each pair of sentences. Then write the appropriate word or phrase from those given in parentheses.

1. Space probes have analyzed the soil and atmosphere of other planets.
   However
   _____ , scientists still have no definite proof of other living things in the solar system. **(Finally, However)**

2. The United States is ''home'' to some of the world's most popular sports.
   For example
   _____ , basketball was invented in Springfield, Massachusetts.   **(For example, After)**

3. The athlete trained hard for years. Eventually _____ , her work paid off. **(Just as, Eventually)**

4. Bees help to pollinate flowers. In addition _____ , they provide honey. **(On the other hand, In addition)**

5. Henry Ford figured out how to make automobiles less expensive.
   As a result
   _____ , more people could afford them.
   (As a result, Before)

6. People in the United States eat beef frequently. In contrast _____ , the Japanese often eat fish. **(In contrast, Though)**

7. George Washington led the Continental Army. In addition _____ , he served as our first President. **(For instance, In addition)**

8. Scientists are continually seeking a cure for cancer. Though _____ progress has been made, no cure has been found yet. **(Though, However)**

Level 8   Unit 12   Research Report   *(Use with pupil book pages 442–445.)*
Skill: Students will choose appropriate transition words or phrases to connect sentences in pairs.

UNIT 12 TEACHER'S ANNOTATED PAGES

Name _____

THE WRITING PROCESS: RESEARCH REPORT

RETEACHING WORKBOOK **96**

Step 5: Proofread

When you proofread, look for mistakes in spelling, capitalization, punctuation, paragraph format, and grammar. Use proofreading marks to make corrections.

If you read *your* ~~you'll~~ essay to us, maybe we can learn from ~~them~~ *it*

Proofreading Marks

¶ Indent.	⌃ Add a comma.	⊙ Add a period.	≡ Capitalize.
∧ Add something.	~ Reverse the order.	ℐ Take out.	/ Make a small letter.
			∨∨ Add quotation marks.

Proofread these paragraphs from a report. There are four capitalization errors, four punctuation errors, two run-on sentences, one spelling error, and one mistake in paragraph format. There are three pronoun errors. Correct these errors. Use a dictionary to check your spelling.

The constellations you see depend on the season and they also depend on where

you are different constellations appear in the Northern and Southern Hemispheres.

The best-known constellation in the Northern Hemisphere is the big Dipper. Two

stars in this constellation point to the North Star. If you watch the big Dipper all

night, it seems to move around the North Star in a circle however, the stars are not

truly moving. Us earthlings are moving. We

Some other constellations are the Big Bear and orion the Hunter. The Big Bear no

longer looks like an animal because some stars have changed they're positions since *their*

it was named Orion is easy to spot in the winter. you will see three bright stars in

a row. They are Orion's belt. Its hard to miss.

Level 8 Unit 12 Research Report   *(Use with pupil book pages 453–454.)*
Skill: Students will proofread paragraphs from a report, correcting mistakes in spelling, capitalization, punctuation, paragraph format, and grammar.

Name _____

THE WRITING PROCESS: RESEARCH REPORT

RETEACHING WORKBOOK **95**

Step 4: Revise

Have I

replaced the dull introduction with an interesting one?

added transition words and phrases?

added details and clarified any confusing pronouns?

crossed out a sentence that gives an opinion?

yes ☐ ☐ ☐ ☐

Revise the following beginning of a research report. Use the check list above to help you. Check off each box when you have finished your revision.
• Use the space above each line and on the sides of the paragraphs for your changes.
• Use the outline section below to check that all the facts have been used in the report.

Sample answers:

I. How Jumbo came to the United States—1882
  A. P. T. Barnum offered to buy from London Zoo
    1. Largest elephant in captivity
    2. Needed special attraction for circus
  B. Protest by British public
    1. Children who had ridden elephant wrote letters
    2. Angry newspaper editorials
  C. Sale completed

The next time you buy a jumbo-sized box of cereal, stop and remember the elephant whose name has become a household word.

I'm going to tell you where the word jumbo came from. You
Jumbo
probably don't know. It was a huge circus elephant brought to

the United States by P. T. Barnum in 1882.
At that time Barnum
Jumbo, the largest elephant in captivity,
He needed a special attraction for his circus. He offered to
London buy it from the zoo. The British public strongly protested. However,
Jumbo
In addition,
Children who had ridden or it wrote letters. I certainly don't
Finally, though,
blame them. Newspaper editors wrote angry editorials. The sale

was completed.

Level 8 Unit 12 Research Report   *(Use with pupil book pages 451–452.)*
Skill: Students will revise part of a research report, writing an interesting introduction, adding transition words, phrases, details, and clarifying pronouns, and crossing out a sentence that gives an opinion.

T46

Name _____

LANGUAGE AND USAGE

RETEACHING
WORKBOOK
97

1 | Prepositions and Prepositional Phrases

▸ A **preposition** shows the relationship between a noun or a pronoun and another word in the sentence.
▸ A **prepositional phrase** includes a preposition, the object or objects of the preposition, and all the modifiers of the object.
▸ When a pronoun is the object of a preposition, use the objective case.

                preposition   object
     Beethoven was one **of the** world's greatest **composers.**
                         prepositional phrase

    preposition   object   object
    Between you and **me,** I like his symphonies best.
           prepositional phrase

Write the prepositional phrases in these sentences.

Example: Beethoven also performed in concerts. _____ **in concerts**

1. Beethoven was born in Germany during the eighteenth century. _____
in Germany, during the eighteenth century

2. We studied scores by him and several other composers of that time.
by him and several other composers, of that time

3. Because of his deafness, Beethoven stopped performing.
Because of his deafness

4. Beethoven broke new ground as a composer. _____ **as a composer**

5. He wrote several extraordinary sonatas for the piano. _____ **for the piano**

6. He wrote his most famous symphony toward the end of his life.
toward the end, of his life

7. Beethoven studied the works of Mozart, Haydn, and other masters.
of Mozart, Haydn, and other masters

8. Beethoven created new forms in place of old ones.
in place of old ones

Level 8   Unit 13   Phrases   *(Use with pupil book pages 462–464.)*
Skill: Students will identify prepositional phrases.

Name _____

LANGUAGE AND USAGE

RETEACHING
WORKBOOK
98

2 | Prepositional Phrases as Modifiers

▸ Prepositional phrases always function as modifiers.
▸ **Adjective phrases** modify nouns or pronouns.
▸ **Adverb phrases** modify verbs, adjectives, or adverbs.

     Adjective Phrase: The exhibit **at the museum** interested the class.

     Adverb Phrase: Our class traveled **to the Metropolitan Museum.**

Write each underlined adjective or adverb phrase and the word that it modifies.

Example: The bus arrived at the museum in the morning.
                at the museum, in the morning—arrived

1. People of all ages visit the Metropolitan Museum.
of all ages—People

2. The students walked into the museum.
into the museum—walked

3. They saw an exhibit of several Renaissance paintings.
of several Renaissance paintings—exhibit

4. For ten minutes Julie observed with special interest one painting.
For ten minutes, with special interest—observed

5. Paintings by Leonardo da Vinci were hung in the special exhibit.
by Leonardo da Vinci—Paintings; in the special exhibit—were hung

6. David could not see enough of the impressionistic paintings.
of the impressionistic paintings—enough

7. One of van Gogh's paintings especially fascinated Alex.
of van Gogh's paintings—One

8. The students were interested in several of the painters.
in several—interested, of the painters—several

Level 8   Unit 13   Phrases   *(Use with pupil book pages 465–466.)*
Skill: Students will identify the words modified by adjective and adverb phrases.

T47

Name _____

4 | Verbals: Participles

▸ A **verbal** is a word that is formed from a verb. Verbals are used as nouns, adjectives, or adverbs.
▸ A **participle** is a verbal used as an adjective.

Blinding lights flood the **crowded** theater.
Those **watching** cannot guess the play's **surprising** outcome.

Write the participles that modify the underlined words in these sentences.

Example: Every year the eighth grade sees an exciting play on Broadway.
exciting

1. Experienced and prepared, the actors always give a superb performance.
   Experienced, prepared

2. Those seated enjoy an unobstructed view of the stage.
   seated, unobstructed

3. Then the students take a guided tour of Manhattan.
   guided

4. Towering buildings and flashing lights are everywhere.
   Towering, flashing

5. They listen to the astounding history of the Brooklyn Bridge.
   astounding

6. The Chrysler Building, striking and shining, delights them.
   striking, shining

7. Later the class enjoys an inspiring concert at Carnegie Hall.
   inspiring

8. Then the students, exhausted and worn, return home by train.
   exhausted, worn

Level 8 Unit 13 Phrases *(Use with pupil book pages 469–470.)*
Skill: Students will identify participles.

Name _____

3 | Choosing the Right Preposition

▸ Use **between** with two people, things, or groups.
▸ Use **among** with more than two people, things, or groups.
▸ Use **beside** to mean "next to."
▸ Use **besides** to mean "in addition to."

The director stood **between** the two characters on-stage.
Among playwrights Shakespeare is perhaps the most famous.
Several attendants sat **beside** the king.
Besides the fool Cordelia remained faithful to King Lear.

Rewrite each sentence, using the correct preposition in parentheses.

Example: (Among, Between) *Hamlet* and *Macbeth*, we chose to see *Hamlet*.
Between *Hamlet* and *Macbeth*, we chose to see *Hamlet*.

1. *Hamlet* is (among, between) Shakespeare's best plays.
   Hamlet is among Shakespeare's best plays.

2. (Beside, Besides) a wonderful plot, the play has great dialogue.
   Besides a wonderful plot, the play has great dialogue.

3. On the way to the play, I sat (beside, besides) Jennifer.
   On the way to the play, I sat beside Jennifer.

4. We had memorized a dialogue (among, between) Hamlet and his mother.
   We had memorized a dialogue between Hamlet and his mother.

5. Sitting (among, between) our classmates, we acted out that dialogue.
   Sitting among our classmates, we acted out that dialogue.

6. We acted out two other dialogues (beside, besides) that one.
   We acted out two other dialogues besides that one.

7. (Among, Between) the two of us, we forgot several lines.
   Between the two of us, we forgot several lines.

8. Finally, our bus arrived and parked (beside, besides) the theater.
   Finally, our bus arrived and parked beside the theater.

Level 8 Unit 13 Phrases *(Use with pupil book pages 467–468.)*
Skill: Students will use the prepositions *between, among, beside,* and *besides* correctly.

Name _____

RETEACHING WORKBOOK 102

LANGUAGE AND USAGE

6 | Verbals: Gerunds

▸ A **gerund** is the present participle of a verb used as a noun.
▸ A gerund functions in all of the ways that a noun does.

  Subject: Jogging is my favorite sport.
  Direct Object: I like **jogging**.
  Object of Preposition: Now is a good time for **jogging**.
  Predicate Noun: My favorite sport is **jogging**.

Write the gerunds in these sentences. Write *none* if a sentence does not have a gerund.

Example: In the spring and summer, Sharon enjoys canoeing.
         canoeing

1. Hiking is Fred's favorite summer activity.
   Hiking

2. Golf and tennis are good ways of relaxing.
   relaxing

3. Terry goes to a nearby rink and teaches skating.
   skating

4. Running is a convenient sport for many people.
   Running

5. A sport that takes courage and skill is skiing.
   skiing

6. At the community pool, Nancy practices diving and swimming.
   diving, swimming

7. Tim and Denise have a running argument about spectator sports.
   none

8. Gloria's favorite spectator sport is sailing.
   sailing

Level 8 Unit 13 Phrases   (Use with pupil book pages 473–474.)
Skill: Students will identify gerunds.

Name _____

RETEACHING WORKBOOK 101

LANGUAGE AND USAGE

5 | Participial Phrases

▸ A **participial phrase** is a participle and its accompanying words.
▸ Participial phrases may contain direct objects, prepositional phrases, and adverbs.

  Reading about the subject first, Ann wrote about Thomas Jefferson.

Write the participial phrase in each sentence.

Example: Raised in Virginia, Jefferson later became its governor.
         Raised in Virginia

1. Studying law in Virginia, Thomas Jefferson heard Patrick Henry speak.
   Studying law in Virginia

2. Jefferson, elected to the House of Burgesses, served faithfully.
   elected to the House of Burgesses

3. Being an excellent architect, he designed his home, Monticello.
   Being an excellent architect

4. Rejecting British views, Jefferson insisted on a colonial government.
   Rejecting British views

5. Writing for the Continental Congress, he drafted the Declaration of Independence.
   Writing for the Continental Congress

6. Making few changes, the Congress adopted the Declaration.
   Making few changes

7. Jefferson, admired by many, became Vice President.
   admired by many

8. Inaugurated in Washington, Jefferson later became the third President.
   Inaugurated in Washington

Level 8 Unit 13 Phrases   (Use with pupil book pages 471–472.)
Skill: Students will identify participial phrases.

T49

Name _____

LANGUAGE AND USAGE

RETEACHING WORKBOOK 103

7 | Gerund Phrases

▶ A gerund phrase can be a subject, a direct object, an object of a preposition, or a predicate noun.
▶ Use a possessive noun or a possessive pronoun before a gerund.

Subject: **Thinking of a story** takes effort.
Direct Object: Tom began **his thinking about a plot.**
Object of Preposition: Before **starting his story,** he read others.
Predicate Noun: Tom's difficulty was **creating a setting.**

A. Write each gerund phrase and underline the gerund.

Example: Creating a believable story took some time.
Creating **a believable story**

1. Describing the main character was easy for Tom.
   Describing **the main character**

2. Tom began outlining a very rough plot.
   outlining **a very rough plot**

3. After writing the first few paragraphs, Tom stopped.
   writing **the first few paragraphs**

B. Write each sentence, using the correct possessive noun or pronoun in parentheses.

Example: (Tom, Tom's) writing a novel might earn him some fame.
Tom's writing a novel might earn him some fame.

4. He listened to (our, us) discussing the plot.
   He listened to our discussing the plot.

5. He did not like (Sarah, Sarah's) retelling of the story.
   He did not like Sarah's retelling of the story.

6. A (reviewer's, reviewer) criticizing the story did not hurt his feelings.
   A reviewer's criticizing the story did not hurt his feelings.

Level 8 Unit 13 Phrases (Use with pupil book pages 475–477.)
Skill: Students will identify gerund phrases and will use possessive nouns or possessive pronouns in gerund phrases.

Name _____

LANGUAGE AND USAGE

RETEACHING WORKBOOK 104

8 | Verbals: Infinitives

▶ An **infinitive** is formed with the word *to* and the base form of the verb.
▶ An infinitive can be used as a noun, an adjective, or an adverb.

Noun: Dana likes **to read.**
Adjective: Novels are good books **to read.**
Adverb: Most newspapers are easy **to read.**

Write the infinitives in these sentences. Write *none* if the sentence does not have an infinitive.

Example: A good book can be a way to explore.   to explore

1. To communicate is the aim of most authors.   **To communicate**
2. To read is a way to grow.   **To read, to grow**
3. A long novel is not necessarily a hard one to follow.   **to follow**
4. Lending a good book to a friend can be very satisfying.   **none**
5. If you want nothing except to escape, read a fantasy adventure.   **to escape**
6. If you want to learn, read a more serious book.   **to learn**
7. Whether a book is light or serious, read to understand.   **to understand**
8. For some books a quick way to read is to skim.   **to read, to skim**
9. If you are willing to concentrate, a difficult book is worthwhile.   **to concentrate**
10. Some books are good enough to reread.   **to reread**

Level 8 Unit 13 Phrases (Use with pupil book pages 478–479.)
Skill: Students will identify infinitives.

T50

Name _____

RETEACHING WORKBOOK 106

LANGUAGE AND USAGE

10 | Combining Sentences: Phrases

▶ You can combine sentences by using prepositional phrases, participial phrases, gerund phrases, or infinitive phrases.

Two Sentences: I read that book. It is by Charles Dickens.
Prepositional Phrase: I read that book **by Charles Dickens**.
Two Sentences: Bob Cratchit was a bookkeeper. Scrooge employed him.
Participial Phrase: Bob Cratchit was a bookkeeper **employed by Scrooge**.
Two Sentences: Bob Cratchit carried Tiny Tim. Cratchit enjoyed it.
Gerund Phrase: Bob Cratchit enjoyed **carrying Tiny Tim**.
Two Sentences: Cratchit needed more money. It would help Tiny Tim.
Infinitive Phrase: Cratchit needed more money **to help Tiny Tim**.

Use the kind of phrase named in parentheses to combine each pair of sentences.

Example: The story takes place long ago. It takes place in London. **(prepositional)**
The story takes place long ago in London.

Sample answers:

1. Cratchit worked hard. He did it to support his family. **(infinitive)**
   Cratchit worked hard to support his family.

2. Scrooge clung to his money. This was his only pleasure. **(gerund)**
   Clinging to his money was Scrooge's only pleasure.

3. Scrooge had dreams. They were about his past, present, and future. **(prepositional)**
   Scrooge had dreams about his past, present, and future.

4. Marley appeared in Scrooge's dreams. He brought Scrooge a warning. **(infinitive)**
   Marley appeared in Scrooge's dreams to bring Scrooge a warning.

5. Scrooge decided to change. He was scared by his dreams. **(participial)**
   Scared by his dreams, Scrooge decided to change.

6. Scrooge arrived at the Cratchits'. He was carrying gifts. **(participial)**
   Carrying gifts, Scrooge arrived at the Cratchits'.

Level 8 Unit 13 Phrases *(Use with pupil book pages 482–483.)*
Skill: Students will combine sentences, using four kinds of phrases.

Name _____

RETEACHING WORKBOOK 105

LANGUAGE AND USAGE

9 | Infinitive Phrases

▶ An **infinitive phrase** consists of an infinitive and words that complete its meaning.
▶ An infinitive phrase acts as a noun, an adjective, or an adverb.

Noun: **To ask for money and ships** took courage.
Adjective: Columbus was the first person **to attempt the voyage**.
Adverb: He was eager **to reach the Far East**.

Write the infinitive phrase in each sentence.

Example: To make the voyage, Columbus needed ships and supplies.
To make the voyage

1. The first task was to ask a king or queen for the funds.
   to ask a king or queen for the funds

2. Most rulers were not prepared to take such a risk.
   to take such a risk

3. Like most explorers Columbus was not one to accept defeat.
   to accept defeat

4. To find an easy route to rich islands was his goal.
   To find an easy route to rich islands

5. Explorers sailed to gain wealth and fame.
   to gain wealth and fame

6. They wanted to explore new worlds.
   to explore new worlds

7. The explorers were brave to face the unknown.
   to face the unknown

8. They did not have accurate maps to guide them safely.
   to guide them safely

9. Some explorers were not sturdy enough to survive the hardships.
   to survive the hardships

10. Others lived to enjoy the glory of their discoveries.
    to enjoy the glory of their discoveries

Level 8 Unit 13 Phrases *(Use with pupil book pages 480–481.)*
Skill: Students will identify infinitive phrases.

T51

Name _____

LANGUAGE AND USAGE

1 Independent and Subordinate Clauses

RETEACHING WORKBOOK **107**

▶ A **clause** is a group of words that has a subject and a predicate.
▶ An **independent clause** expresses a complete thought.
▶ A **subordinate clause** does not state a complete thought and cannot stand alone as a sentence.

Phrase	**Clause**
	subject predicate
after many cold days	**after** the weather turned cold
Independent Clause	**Subordinate Clause**
the ground hardens	**when** the ground hardens

A. Label each clause *independent* or *subordinate*.

Example: when the weather gets cold enough   subordinate

1. the snow falls steadily   **independent**

2. the wind blows through the leafless trees   **independent**

3. before the winter begins   **subordinate**

4. while the deer look for food in the snow   **subordinate**

5. the wind finally dies down   **independent**

B. Label each group of words *phrase* or *clause*.

Example: before the cold weather comes   clause

6. as the sky clears   **clause**

7. since the first snowfall   **phrase**

8. before winter actually begins   **clause**

9. since winter is approaching   **clause**

10. until a heavy snowstorm   **phrase**

11. after people shovel their walks   **clause**

12. after weeks of low temperatures   **phrase**

13. until the lake freezes   **clause**

14. before the end of February   **phrase**

Level 8 Unit 14 Clauses   (Use with pupil book pages 502–503.)
Skill: Students will identify phrases, independent clauses, and subordinate clauses.

Name _____

LANGUAGE AND USAGE

2 Adjective Clauses

RETEACHING WORKBOOK **108**

▶ An **adjective clause** modifies a noun or a pronoun.
▶ A **relative pronoun** such as *who*, *which*, or *that* usually introduces an adjective clause.
▶ The words *where* and *when* also introduce adjective clauses.

The woman **who cares for the cats** gives them milk.
My cat, **which was a stray cat**, is now a good house pet.
The cat **that Tom owns** is a special breed.

Write the adjective clause in each sentence.

Example: The house cat, which is related to wild cats, is quite tame.

   which is related to wild cats

1. The amount of food that a cat needs depends on its age and size.

   that a cat needs

2. Those who own cats soon learn their pets' likes and dislikes.

   who own cats

3. Cats usually like dairy products, which are good for them.

   which are good for them

4. The joints that cats have give them agility.

   that cats have

5. Cats' paws, which are cushioned by pads, enable them to move quietly.

   which are cushioned by pads

6. The time when a cat's vision is best is at night.

   when a cat's vision is best

7. Scientists who study cats are also interested in their vocal cords.

   who study cats

8. The sounds that a cat makes include purring and growling.

   that a cat makes

Level 8 Unit 14 Clauses   (Use with pupil book pages 504–505.)
Skill: Students will identify adjective clauses.

LANGUAGE AND USAGE

3 | Adjective Clauses with *who, whom,* and *whose*

> ▸ Use **who** when the relative pronoun is the subject of the adjective clause.
> ▸ Use **whom** when the relative pronoun is the direct object or the object of a preposition in the adjective clause.
> ▸ Use **whose** when the relative pronoun shows possession.
>
> **Subject:** Frost is a poet **who** often wrote about New England.
> **Direct Object:** Frost is a poet **whom** many people admire.
> **Object of Preposition:** Frost is a poet for **whom** I have great respect.
> **Possessive Pronoun:** Frost is a poet **whose** poems are widely read today.

Write each sentence, using the correct relative pronoun in parentheses.

Example: Our teacher, (who, whom) admires Frost, read his poems.

Our teacher, who admires Frost, read his poems.

1. Frost was a poet (who, whose) was often optimistic about people.
   Frost was a poet who was often optimistic about people.

2. He was a poet (who, whose) words touched many readers.
   He was a poet whose words touched many readers.

3. Frost, (who, whose) poems contain insight, wrote about human nature.
   Frost, whose poems contain insight, wrote about human nature.

4. The poet, (who, whom) critics still study today, wrote about New England.
   The poet, whom critics still study today, wrote about New England.

5. Frost, (whom, who) was born in San Francisco, moved to New England.
   Frost, who was born in San Francisco, moved to New England.

6. The characters about (who, whom) he wrote live today in his poems.
   The characters about whom he wrote live today in his poems.

7. The poet, (whose, who) was also a farmer, created images of rural life.
   The poet, who was also a farmer, created images of rural life.

8. Farmers, with (whose, whom) Frost identified, often speak in his poems.
   Farmers, with whom Frost identified, often speak in his poems.

LANGUAGE AND USAGE

4 | Essential and Nonessential Clauses

> ▸ An adjective clause is either essential or nonessential.
> ▸ An **essential clause** identifies the noun or the pronoun modified. It is not set off by commas.
> ▸ A **nonessential clause** gives extra information about the noun or the pronoun it modifies. It is set off by commas.
>
> **Essential Clause:** Anyone **who visits St. Louis** will like it.
> **Nonessential Clause:** Missouri, **which has many farms,** is quite pretty.

Write each adjective clause. Label each clause *essential* or *nonessential.*

Example: Mark Twain, who was a famous novelist, came from Missouri.

who was a famous novelist—nonessential

1. Missouri, which is a colorful state, is in the Midwest.
   which is a colorful state—nonessential

2. The arch that is in St. Louis looks impressive.
   that is in St. Louis—essential

3. St. Louis and Kansas City, which are both in Missouri, are large cities.
   which are both in Missouri—nonessential

4. Trails that were crucial to western expansion began in Missouri.
   that were crucial to western expansion—essential

5. Lewis and Clark, who explored the West, set out from St. Louis.
   who explored the West—nonessential

6. Those who traveled the Mississippi usually rode on steamboats.
   who traveled the Mississippi—essential

7. Harry Truman, who was born in Missouri, was the state's most famous politician.
   who was born in Missouri—nonessential

8. A famous scientist who came from Missouri was George Washington Carver.
   who came from Missouri—essential

Name _____

RETEACHING WORKBOOK

LANGUAGE AND USAGE

5 Adverb Clauses

- An **adverb clause** is a subordinate clause used as an adverb.
- A **subordinating conjunction** introduces an adverb clause.
- Use a comma after an adverb clause that begins a sentence.

  While we were in Canada, we toured Montreal. (modifies verb *toured*)
  It was larger **than we expected**. (modifies the adjective *larger*)
  I thought about that trip long **after I returned**. (modifies the adverb *long*)

Write each adverb clause and the word or words that it modifies.

Example: We traveled to Montreal even though it was raining.
  even though it was raining—traveled

1. Whenever I see a map of Canada, I think of our trip to Montreal.
   Whenever I see a map of Canada—think

2. We reached the border after we traveled through New York State.
   after we traveled through New York State—reached

3. Wherever we went, the people in Montreal greeted us pleasantly.
   Wherever we went—greeted

4. We were delighted when we saw the botanical gardens.
   when we saw the botanical gardens—were delighted

5. If you visit Montreal, see Mount Royal Park.
   If you visit Montreal—see

6. It is colder in Montreal than it is in most of the United States.
   than it is in most of the United States—colder

7. Before we visited the shops in Montreal, we saw several churches.
   Before we visited the shops in Montreal—saw

8. We enjoyed the visit more than we had expected.
   than we had expected—more

Level 8 Unit 14 Clauses (Use with pupil book pages 510–512.)
Skill: Students will identify adverb clauses and the words that they modify.

Name _____

RETEACHING WORKBOOK

LANGUAGE AND USAGE

6 Noun Clauses

- A **noun clause** is a subordinate clause that acts as a noun.
- Use *who* and *whoever* as subjects in noun clauses.
- Use *whom* and *whomever* as objects in noun clauses.

  Subject: *What is wrong with the car* is a mystery.
  Direct Object: I do not know *what the matter is*.
  Indirect Object: Give *whoever does the repairs* the keys.
  Object of Preposition: I am prepared for *whatever must be done*.
  Predicate Noun: A complete tune-up is *what the car needs*.

A. Write the noun clause in each sentence.

Example: Whoever did these repairs did a good job.
  Whoever did these repairs

1. Gasoline, air, and electricity are what turns the car's engine.
   what turns the car's engine

2. A mechanic knows how the engine works.
   how the engine works

3. The carburetor mixes air with whatever fuels the car.
   whatever fuels the car

4. That the carburetor needed adjustment was apparent.
   That the carburetor needed adjustment

B. Rewrite each sentence, using the correct relative pronoun in parentheses.

Example: Tell me (who, whom) is the best mechanic.
  Tell me who is the best mechanic.

5. (Whoever, Whomever) repairs cars must understand how they work.
   Whoever repairs cars must understand how they work.

6. (Whoever, Whomever) you call should be able to answer your questions.
   Whomever you call should be able to answer your questions.

Level 8 Unit 14 Clauses (Use with pupil book pages 513–515.)
Skill: Students will identify noun clauses and will use relative pronouns correctly.

T54

Name _____

LANGUAGE AND USAGE

RETEACHING WORKBOOK 113

7 | Combining Sentences: Subordinate Clauses

▶ You can use subordinate clauses to combine sentences with related ideas into a single complex sentence.

Two Sentences: New York is an exciting place. Most visitors think so.
Noun Clause: Most visitors think **that New York is an exciting place**.
Two Sentences: Joan took a trip to New York. She enjoyed it.
Adjective Clause: Joan took a trip to New York, **which she enjoyed**.
Two Sentences: Joan liked New York. She hoped to return.
Adverb Clause: **Because Joan liked New York,** she hoped to return.

Combine each pair of simple sentences into a complex sentence, using the type of clause and the conjunction shown in parentheses. Use commas where they are needed.

Example: We went to New York. We wanted to see skyscrapers. (adverb—because)

We went to New York because we wanted to see skyscrapers.

Sample answers:

1. We learned about New York. It was interesting. (noun—what)
   What we learned about New York was interesting.

2. President Roosevelt was once governor of New York. It came as a surprise to some of us. (noun—that)
   That President Roosevelt was once governor of New York came as a surprise to some of us.

3. We admired Albany's skyline. We crossed the Hudson River. (adverb—as)
   We admired Albany's skyline as we crossed the Hudson River.

4. We visited the Eastman House. It is in Rochester. (adjective—which)
   We visited the Eastman House, which is in Rochester.

5. New York City is fascinating. You can also see exciting things in other parts of the state. (adverb—although)
   Although New York City is fascinating, you can also see exciting things in other parts of the state.

Level 8 Unit 14 Clauses (Use with pupil book pages 516–517.)
Skill: Students will combine sentences, using subordinate clauses.

Index

Abbreviations, 71
Adjective clauses, 108–110
Adjective phrases, 98
Adjectives, comparative forms of, 52; distinguishing from adverbs, 56; identifying, 51; predicate, 38, 51; proper, 51, 64
Adverb clauses, identifying, 111
Adverb phrases, 98
Adverbs, comparative forms of, 54; distinguishing from adjectives, 56; identifying, 53; negatives, 55
Agreement, indefinite pronouns, 86; pronouns and antecedents, 82; subject-verb, 32, 40–42
Apostrophes, 72
Appositives, 21, 66

Beginnings, revising, 15, 49; writing, 11

Capitalization, of abbreviations, 71; of proper adjectives, 64; of proper nouns, 17, 64; of quotations, 68; of sentences, 63; of titles, 69
Characters, 47; revising, 49
Clauses, 8, 107–113
Commas, 10, 63, 65–67
Comparison and contrast, 23–27
Composition skills. (*See individual skill listings.*)
Conclusions, 93; revising, 79
Conjunctions, 7, 111
Contractions, 72

Description, 57–61
Details, in outlines, 92; revising, 15, 26, 49, 60, 95; supporting, 12, 23, 57
Dialogue, 13; punctuating, 68; revising, 49
Direct objects, 37

Endings, writing, 14–15
Exact words, 58; revising, 26, 60

Gerund phrases, 103, 106
Gerunds, 102

Homophones, 81

Indirect objects, 37
Infinitive phrases, 105–106
Infinitives, 104
Intensifiers, 53
Interjections, 10, 63
Introductions, 93; revising, 95

Letters, 67, 70, 75–80

Main idea, 23
Metaphors, 58; revising, 95

Negatives, 55
Nominative case, 83
Note-taking, 91
Noun clauses, 112
Nouns, abstract, 17; appositives, 21, 66; common, 17; compound, 18; concrete, 17; identifying, 17–18; of direct address, 66; plural, 19; possessive, 20; predicate, 38; proper, 17, 64
Numbers, 71–72

Objective case, 83
Objects, direct, 37; indirect, 37; of prepositions, 97
Opinions, 76; revising, 79, 95
Order, in paragraphs, 45, 59, 78; revising, 60, 79; in sentences, 4, 42
Outlines, 92

Paragraphs, comparison and contrast, 25; description, 57–61; main idea, 23; narrative, 11–16; organizing, 25, 59; persuasive, 77–78; topic sentences, 24; transitions, 94
Participial phrases, 101, 106
Participles, 100
Personal narrative, 11–16
Persuasive letter, 75–80
Phrases, combining sentences with, 106; gerund, 103; infinitive, 105; participial, 101, prepositional, 97–98
Plot, 45
Point of view, 48–49, 57, 60
Predicates, complete, 2; compound, 5; simple, 3
Prepositional phrases, 97–98, 106, 107
Prepositions, 97; misused, 99
Pronouns, antecedents, 82; case forms of, 83; demonstrative, 85; in incomplete comparisons, 88; indefinite, 86; intensive, 87; interrogative, 84; object, 83; personal, 81; possessive, 81; reflexive, 87; relative, 108; subject, 83; *we, us*, 88
Proofreading, 16, 27, 50, 61, 80, 96
Punctuation, apostrophes, 72; colons, 70; commas, 10, 63, 65–67; dashes, 73; exclamation points, 1, 63; hyphens, 73; parentheses, 73; periods, 1, 63, 71; question marks, 1, 63, 68; quotation marks, 68; semicolons, 70; underlining, 69

Quotations, direct, 68

Research reports, 89–96
Revising, 15, 26, 49, 60, 79, 95

Sentence fragments, 9
Sentences, capitalization of, 63; combining, 6, 21, 106, 113; complex, 8; compound, 6, 65; inverted order in, 4, 42; punctuating, 1, 63; run-on, 9; simple, 6; topic, 24; types of, 1, 63
Setting, 46; revising, 49
Similes, 58; revising, 60
Spelling, irregular verbs, 33–34; plural nouns, 19
Stories, 45–50; beginnings, 11; characters, 47; descriptive language, 58; details, 12, 23, 57; dialogue, 13; endings, 14; plot, 45; point of view, 48; proofreading, 50; revising, 49; setting, 46
Subjects, agreement with verb, 32, 40–42, 86; identifying, 2–5

Titles, 68–69
Topic sentences, 24; revising, 26, 79
Topics, narrowing, 89
Transitions, 94–95

Usage, *accept, except*, 44; adjectives, forms of comparison, 52; adverbs, forms of comparison, 54; *affect, effect*, 44; agreement, subject-verb, 40–42; *among, between*, 99; antecedents, 82; *be, have, do*, 32; *beside, besides*, 99; clauses, 107–113; conjunctions, 7; demonstrative pronouns, 85; distinguishing between adjectives and adverbs, 56; gerund phrases, 103; incomplete comparisons, 88; indefinite pronouns, 86; interrogative pronouns, 84; irregular verbs, 33–34; *lie, lay*, 43; negatives, 55; participial phrases, 101; possessive pronouns, 81; prepositions, 99; pronouns, case, 83; reflexive and intensive pronouns, 87; *rise, raise*, 43; *we, us*, 88

Verb phrases, 30
Verbals, 100, 102, 104
Verbs, action, 29; active voice, 39; agreement with subject, 32, 40–42, 86; *be, have, do*, 32; helping, 30; intransitive, 36; irregular, 33–34; linking, 29, 38; main, 30; of being, 29; passive voice, 39; principal parts of, 33–34; progressive forms, 35; tenses, 31–32; transitive, 36

Words, exact, 26, 58, 60; order, 59; sense, 60; transitional, 95

T56

Notes

Notes

Notes